Secrets of
CHINESE
ASTROLOGY

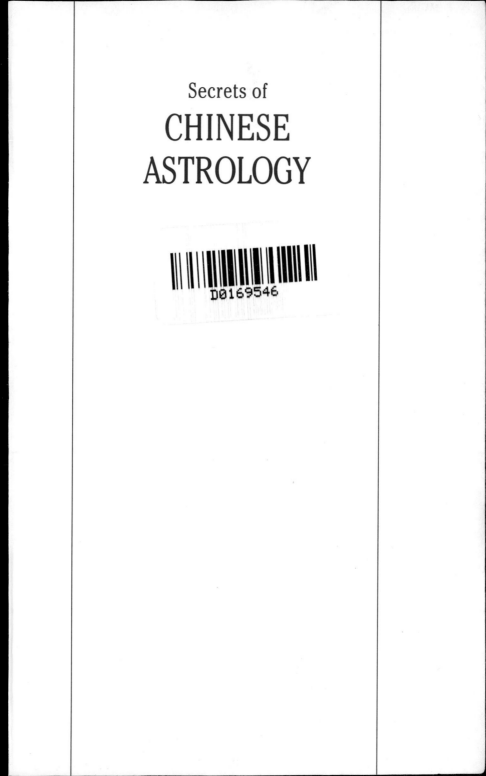

D0169546

Secrets of
CHINESE
ASTROLOGY

✳

A Handbook
for Self-Discovery

by Kwan Lau

First edition, 1994
Second printing, 1995

Tengu Books

420 Madison Avenue, 15th Floor
New York, N.Y. 10017

Library of Congress Cataloging-in-Publication Data

The secrets of Chinese astrology / by Kwan Lau
     p.   cm.
        ISBN 0-8348-0306-2 (pbk.): $9.95
       1. Astrology, Chinese.   I. Title
BF1714.C5K93 1994   133.5—dc20   93-44024
                                           CIP

Printed in the U.S.A.
ISBN 0-8348-0306-2

CONTENTS

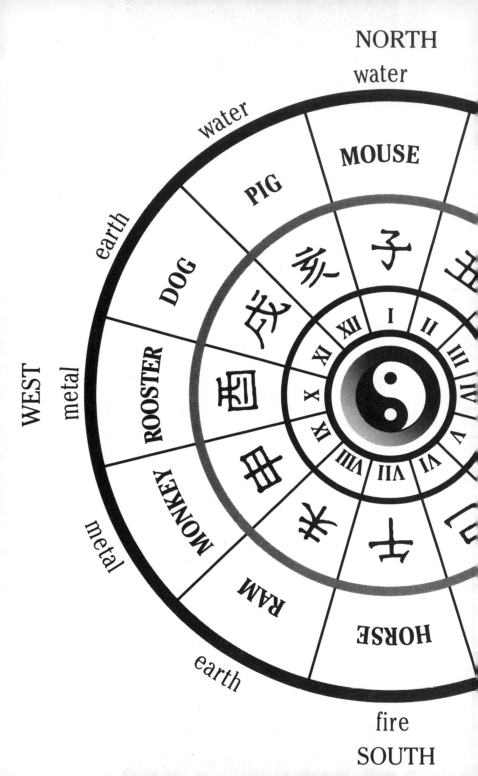

INTRODUCTION

HOW TO
USE
THIS BOOK

WHERE DO I BEGIN?

In Chinese astrology, the fundamental category is the entire year of birth, in an endlessly recurring cycle of Twelve Animal Years (often called the Chinese zodiac), followed in importance by the lunar month, or moon. Since the traditional Chinese lunisolar calendar is very different from the Western calendar, you will first need to consult the CALENDRICAL CONVERSION CHART on pp. 30–45. Make a note of both your animal year and birth moon; then turn to the appropriate animal year chapter to receive your Chinese astrological reading, including the important "associations" for each.

WHAT ARE ASSOCIATIONS?

The first section in the animal year chapters— Associations—will be new to readers familiar only with Western astrology. This is because Chinese astrology involves much more than just the the movements of the heavenly bodies. The associations of each year include: the animal for that year; a special Chinese numbering character from what are called the Twelve Earthly Branches; one of the Five Elements from ancient Chinese alchemical theory; one of the Seven Main Stars, and so on. Each of these associations illuminates a different aspect of the whole person and contributes to our understanding of him or her.

WHAT CAN I LEARN FROM THIS BOOK?

The Associations section in each animal year chapter provides the basic Chinese astrological reading for people born in that year. This is followed by a more Western-style analysis of different aspects of the person's character, lifestyle, and emotional makeup.

Since the lunar birth months have a significant influence on the persons born in them, a special section discusses how the birth moon affects and modifies the basic reading for the animal year. Individual sections on health, money, career, and love follow, providing a useful look at these important issues and some practical suggestions for the reader.

The last section in each chapter is a sketch of the outlook for relationships with people born in all the different animal years, primarily concerned with love and romance, but also applicable to friendship and business relations.

WHAT ABOUT SPECIFIC QUESTIONS?

The YI JING COIN ORACLES chapter on pp.184–205 is a special supplement to this book which allows you to access the practical wisdom of the *Yi Jing*—the classical Chinese book of divination—and apply it to specific questions or problems you are facing in your own life.

HOW SERIOUSLY SHOULD I TAKE IT?

Sometimes as you read this book you will feel like saying, "Wow, that's true!" When that happens, it probably *is* true. But what seems wrong to you is also probably wrong *for* you, in part because the presentation here necessarily simplifies the immensely complex tradition of Chinese astrology. If you wish to learn more about the origins, theory, and concepts of this tradition, read THE CYCLES OF CHINESE ASTROLOGY in the section following this one. Otherwise, just dive in! But keep in mind one important fact: Chinese astrology is not meant to tell you anything you don't already know—it is to help you pull what you *do* know out of your subconscious. Don't make any serious decisions based on what you read here—history is full of stories of lovers separated and battles lost because someone took an astrologer's advice too literally, and you should not let that happen to you.

THE
CYCLES
OF
CHINESE
ASTROLOGY

Chinese astrology differs from Western astrology not only in its basic concepts—animal years, character cycles, and so on—but also in its intellectual spirit.

Chinese astrology is not really a predictive science, nor does it claim to be. No serious Chinese astrologer would assert, as many Western astrologers do, that knowing the date and time of someone's birth makes it possible to predict that person's future life and destiny with any degree of accuracy. Chinese astrology is instead a kind of practical philosophy, based on the idea that we can make the most of our unknowable fate by seeking to harmonize our thought and behavior within the broad contexts of heaven, earth, and humanity, nourished by the life force, or *qi*.

Living, in this view, is like playing in an orchestra. The beauty of the music depends on each musician adjusting pitch, rhythm, and volume to the structure of the piece, the qualities of the instrument, and the performance of the other players. In the same way, happiness in life depends on each of us making our own contribution in a way that harmonizes with the entire context of our circumstances and relationships.

The task of astrology is to provide a kind of music theory for living. Ancient Chinese science—especially calendrical science and astronomy—defined a set of patterns in time, heavenly space, earthly space, and the relations among the "ten thousand things" of the universe. It is not believed that these patterns determine each other, as the patterns of the stars in Western astrology are supposed to do. Rather, under the assumption that all things must ultimately be in harmony, it is believed that there are systematic correspondences among the different realms and categories of existence, so that understanding the nature of one set of patterns yields ways of understanding the potential of another set.

This is why, in modern terms, Chinese astrology is not a predictive science like physics or a historical science like evolutionary biology, but an interpretive science like the most advanced anthropology. It maps the multifarious behavior of the human individual against correspondences among cosmic patterns as a way of trying to explore each person's uniqueness as an element in the general pattern, a part of a greater whole. On a practical level, the idea is to use such understanding both to one's own advantage and for the greater harmony of society. Much of the "science" in Chinese astrology may be outdated, but the patterns themselves seem to transcend this, and when you apply them to your own life and the lives of those you are close to, you will often be amazed at how trenchantly they seem to fit.

The Western term "astrology" (theory of the stars) is not really a good name for this discipline, for despite its heavy use of astronomical calculations, the Chinese system involves much more than the stars. People are at its center, and the measurement of time is its main yardstick; it might better be known as "calendrical psychology." However, we will use the more commonly employed term here, for the sake of convenience and familiarity.

Chinese astrology might even be considered as a kind of popular art, in the way it seeks not the facts but deeper ways of understanding them. It is built chiefly on a web of mythological and literary associations, a kind of personalized narrative of the stars and of the symbolic ideograms and animals. As a psychological "science" it seems eccentric, sometimes even inconsistent, and the kinds of insight it offers are very much those we associate with art and mythology: the flash of recognition, the sudden epiphany. It is, as Claude Lévi-Strauss has said of mythology in general, "good for thinking with." This may be the secret of its survival over more than twenty-six hundred years, especially in this science-obsessed century, for it lives on in the hearts and minds of the common people, regardless of scientific evolution and technological progress.

HISTORICAL ORIGINS

Chinese civilization developed in the rich bottomland of the Yellow River valley, where the harvests are magnificent under good conditions but frequent severe flooding or drought leads to uncertainty and sometimes catastrophe. The earliest emperors had a primarily priestly function; they were supposed to obtain divine favor in the form of good weather and moderate rainfall, which is why they were said to possess the Mandate of Heaven as long as things went well, and to have lost it in times of disaster.

Ancient legends show that they did not limit themselves to prayer, but gave nature some practical assistance as well, organizing vast hydraulic projects to control flooding and irrigate more and more fields. By the time of the the Shang Dynasty (1500–1100 BC) court officials specializing in these matters had developed a very sophisticated understanding of astronomy, calendrical cycles, and weather patterns, and were documenting heavenly, seasonal, and agricultural events: the movements of sun, moon, and stars; the occurrence of eclipses and meteor showers; the solstices and equinoxes; the tides and the cycles of flood and drought.

These officials, ancestors of the scholarly mandarins of later Chinese history, were a combination of priest, scientist and politician, charged with maintaining the stability and welfare of the realm and keeping and protecting the royal power against social upheaval and dynastic change. They needed to know as much about people as they did about the stars and the seasons. Their refined ideas on the relations between ruler and minister (developed with the purpose of keeping their own heads intact!) are at the root of classical Chinese philosophy, as is clear from reading Laozi (Lao-tse) and Kongzi (Confucius). Their theories of human nature, based on the idea that patterns of thought and behavior could be found to correspond to the patterns of seasonal change and star movement that they knew so well, are the origin of Chinese astrology.

It took many centuries for this system of thought to develop fully; in particular the aspect that is most familiar today, the cycle of the twelve animals, was probably not introduced until toward the end of the Han Dynasty (206 BC–AD 221). But its fundamental principles were fully formed as early as the sixth century BC, when the *Book of Changes* or *Yi Jing* (*I Ching* in the old Wade-Giles transliteration) was written. This book is best known today as a manual for divination, but centuries of interpretation of its mysterious text have found in it a full-blown metaphysics upon which some of the most profound aspects of Chinese thought are based.

CYCLES IN ANCIENT CHINESE ALCHEMY AND ASTRONOMY

The universe is truly one and indivisible, according to the *Yi Jing,* but any aspect of it regarded from a specific point of view makes it appear dual, divided between the dark, cool, soft, female *yin* force and the bright, hot, hard, male *yang* force. In the quiet, cool midnight hour, for example, it appears that the yin force has taken over the universe, while at the hot and noisy hour of noon yin seems to have been obliterated by the yang; but when we consider the cycle of the day as a whole, and understand that the end of one cycle is the beginning of another, we see that yin and yang always balance each other out, and that their contrast is not a conflict but a harmony greater than either, animated by a single force called *qi*.

This picture of a cyclical balance between yin and yang recurring eternally and resolved in ultimate harmony can be applied to a whole multitude of different phenomena: to the cycle of the seasons and the points of the compass (used in China more than a thousand years before it was discovered in the West), to the map of the heavens and the list of fundamental elements, and so on. The great inspiration of Chinese astrology is to see that human life, too, can be seen as such a cycle, or a multiple mapping of different cycles. Before we can discuss this in any detail, however, we need to sketch out some of the more basic cycles.

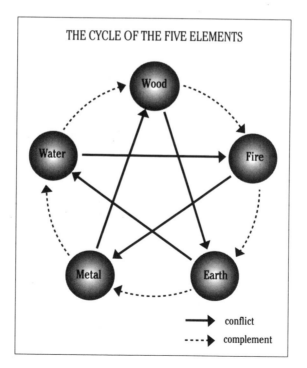

THE CYCLE OF THE FIVE ELEMENTS

All things are composed, according to ancient Chinese theory, of Five Elements that emerge in their turn from the interaction of yin and yang: Wood, the lesser yang, growing out of or declining toward yin and associated with the color green; Fire, the greater or mature yang, associated with red; Earth, in which yin and yang are perfectly balanced, associated with yellow; Metal, the lesser yin, growing out of or declining toward yang and associated with white; and Water, the greater or mature yin, associated with black. (Air is not an element in this system, but constitutes the life force, *qi*, itself.)

The first great mapping of cycles comes between this alchemical world and the astronomical world: each of the Five Elements is associated with one of the five visible planets, as in the table below. These planets, together with the sun and the moon, which represent pure yang and pure yin respectively, comprise the Seven Main Stars, those that move independently of the grid of the fixed stars.

Wood	Jupiter	green	lesser yang
Fire	Mars	red	greater yang
Earth	Saturn	yellow	balance
Metal	Venus	white	lesser yin
Water	Mercury	black	greater yin

Chinese astrology in the proper "star theory" sense of the term is concerned with the relationships of the Seven Main Stars and a starscape composed of twenty-eight major constellations, each with its own auspicious or ominous meaning in terms of the yin-yang balance and the Five Elements. These constellations are called Lodges, or Star-Spirits, and move in and out of Palaces ruled by the Seven Main Stars. Each Palace is associated in turn with one of the twelve moons of the lunar calendar, the Twelve Earthly Branches, and the twelve zodiac animals (the Palaces, Lodges, and their correspondences are listed in the table on p. 20; illustrations of the Lodges and their seasonal associations appear on pp. 18–19).

THE FOUR SEASONS
AND THE TWENTY-EIGHT
STAR LODGES

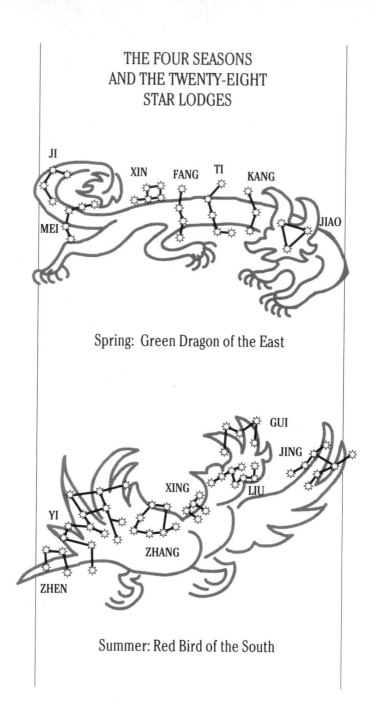

Spring: Green Dragon of the East

Summer: Red Bird of the South

THE FOUR SEASONS
AND THE TWENTY-EIGHT
STAR LODGES

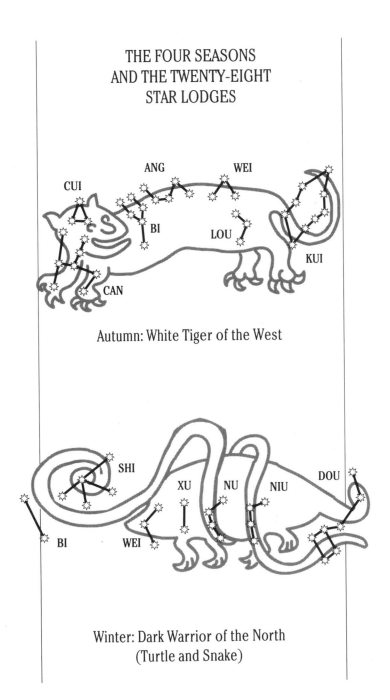

Autumn: White Tiger of the West

Winter: Dark Warrior of the North
(Turtle and Snake)

THE PALACES, LODGES, & THEIR CORRESPONDENCES

Palace	Element	Animal	Lodge	Western Constellations
Saturn	Earth	Mouse	Dou Niu Nu Xu	Sagittarius Aries, Sagittarius Aquarius Aquarius, Equuleus
Saturn	Earth	Ox	Yi (Mei) Ji Dou	Scorpio Sagittarius Sagittarius
Jupiter	Wood	Tiger	Ti Fang Xin Yi (Mei)	Libra Scorpio Antares, Scorpio Scorpio
Mars	Fire	Rabbit	Jiao Kang Ti	Spica, Virgo Virgo Libra
Venus	Metal	Dragon	Yi Zhen Jiao	Crater, Hydra Corvus Spica, Virgo
Mercury	Water	Snake	Xing Zhang Yi	Hydra Hydra Hydra, Crater
Sun	none	Horse	Jing Qui Liu Xing	Gemini Cancer Hydra Hydra
Moon	none	Ram	Can Jing	Orion Gemini
Mercury	Water	Monkey	Ang Bi Cui Jing	Pleiades Hyades, Taurus Orion Orion
Venus	Metal	Rooster	Kui Lou Wei Ang	Andromeda, Pisces Aries Musca Borealis Pleiades
Mars	Fire	Dog	Shi Bi Kui	Pegasus Pegasus, Andromeda Andromeda, Pisces
Jupiter	Water	Pig	Xu Wei Shi	Aquarius, Equuleus Aquarius, Pegasus Pegasus

This aspect of Chinese astrology is similar to Western astrology, except for the fact that the division of stars into Lodges is different from the Western zodiac

Each person is assigned by birth year to a Main Star, and as the various Lodges passes through its Palace, the person is supposed experiences good or bad fortune accordingly. Other stars not included in the Twenty-Eight Lodges also play a role in human destiny, especially the Great Bear, which is the sky-throne of the god Shang Di and the fount of wisdom and good luck, around which the Twenty-Eight Lodges revolve.

The system is probably no more or less useful than Western astrology in helping people to decide when to embark on a project or trip or when to sit tight and stay home. But the uniqueness of Chinese astrology and the other East Asian systems derived from it comes from something entirely different: the way the human element has been incorporated as a variable in its own right. When a person dies, for example, it is believed that his or her heavenly star dies as well, to be replaced with a new-born star!

CHARACTER CYCLES AND TIME

Human culture became inextricably linked to the astrological system through perhaps the greatest achievement of prehistoric Chinese civilization, its ideographic writing system. Twenty-two archaic characters, used for writing numerical sequences and known respectively as the Ten Heavenly Stems and the Twelve Earthly Branches, were organized into cycles of human activity and then mapped against the cycles of natural phenomena as they were understood in ancient times.

The Heavenly Stems are used to number things that come in series of ten. They were associated primarily with the Five Elements, in pairs that linked each element conceptually with both its occurrence in nature and its manifestation in the world of man (see the table of the Heavenly Stems on the following page).

These characters, given here for reference only, play a relatively minor role in the simplified Chinese astrology presented in this book, but are important for understanding the numbering system for the LIFE-SPAN CYCLE presented later in this chapter.

THE TEN HEAVENLY STEMS

Order	Stem	Affinity	Element
1	Jia	trees	Water
2	Yi	hewn timber	Earth
3	Bing	lightning	Wood
4	Ding	burning incense	Wood
5	Wu	hills	Earth
6	Ji	earthenware	Fire
7	Geng	ore	Fire
8	Xin	kettles	Earth
9	Ren	salt water	Metal
10	Gui	fresh water	Metal

Much more important to the psychological aspect of Chinese astrology are the Twelve Earthly Branches, a set of characters that have come to have meanings so complex and so variable according to the context that they are almost like persons, or perhaps deities, in their own right. The Earthly Branches are used to number things that come in series of twelve, especially cycles of time; they are often referred to as the horary cycle, because their original function was to divide the day into twelve 120-minute "hours," starting with the Zi hour, at the period between 11:00 PM and 1:00 AM, when the yin force is at its zenith, and concluding with the Wu hour at the zenith of the yang force. Each of these hours is endowed not only with the specific yin-yang balance indicated by the Earthly Branch character, but also with more human characteristics, developed by association through millennia of use in astrology and other forms of divination.

The Earthly Branches also designate and lend human significance to the months of the year in the Chinese lunisolar calendar and to the cycle of Twelve Animal Years (Year of the

Mouse, Year of the Ox, etc.) that form the Chinese zodiac. Each of the Earthly Branches also has its own elemental, planetary, and directional association as well, as shown in the table below. Understanding this table requires a little background.

THE TWELVE EARTHLY BRANCHES

Order	Branch	Sign	Element	Direction
1	子 Zi	Mouse	Water	N
2	丑 Chou	Ox	Earth	NNE
3	寅 Yin	Tiger	Wood	ENE
4	卯 Mao	Rabbit	Wood	E
5	辰 Chen	Dragon	Earth	ESE
6	巳 Si	Snake	Fire	SSE
7	午 Wu	Horse	Fire	S
8	未 Wei	Ram	Earth	SSW
9	申 Shen	Monkey	Metal	WWS
10	酉 You	Rooster	Metal	W
11	戌 Xu	Dog	Earth	WNW
12	亥 Hai	Pig	Water	NNW

All cultures in which calendrical science has been developed have reckoned both the lunar month (in synodic periods from new moon to new moon of slightly more than 29.5 days, or lunations) and the solar year (consisting of a little more than 365 days from solstice to solstice, or twelve lunations plus about eleven days). Various methods have been developed for reconciling these two very different methods of reckoning time. Europeans, for instance, gradually gave up on the concept of the lunation, creating solar "months" of up to thirty-one days, adding the idea of the quadrennial leap day, and so on.

The Chinese developed a "lunisolar" calendar that retained the synodic month, beginning at the new moon, with the full moon on the fifteenth day, and lasting either twenty-nine ("small" month) or thirty ("big" month) days, according to an alternation laid out centuries in advance through uninterrupted millennia of recordings (generally the only way to find out whether a given month will be big or small is to look at the

Chinese calendar). The year consists of twelve of these lunar months, starting with the second new moon after the winter solstice, plus an intercalary or "leap" thirteenth month added every two or three years (the leap month comes at different times in different years, but is always considered a repetition of whichever month it follows; those who are lucky enough to be born in that month get two birthdays). Thus the individual year is neither solar nor lunar, anywhere from 354 to 384 days long, but over the long run of thirty-three solar years the lunar and solar cycles catch up to one another approximately, and the winter solstice always comes at some point in the eleventh lunar month, the spring equinox in the second, and so forth.

In strictly logical terms, the cycle of months ought to begin parallel to the cycle of hours, with the period of maximum yin around the winter solstice, when the hours of sunlight are at their shortest and weakest. Calculating it this way (although this means starting the New Year with the Yin month, the third of the Earthly Branches cycle) has been a strong tradition, which has influenced Chinese astrology at many points. But the human cycle of months, based on the timetable of farm work, runs differently.

In Chinese agricultural communities, the period of maximum social yin, seen as passivity, is during the couple of weeks before it is time to begin preparing the fields for the spring planting, a time when practically no farm work really needs to be done. The peasants heave a collective sigh of relief as the harvest has lasted them through the winter, and say that they have "eaten the year," rather than the year eaten them; it is in this sense that people say the old year has ended and the new year begun.

So, during the days before the second new moon after the winter solstice, they prepare all kinds of wonderful foods, buy new clothes and furnishings, clean the house until it is spotless and decorate it with auspicious messages in calligraphy on red paper. Then the New Year festivities can begin. In the first days, various kinds of work are forbidden: nobody uses a knife, because this can symbolize quarrels at a time of reconciliation, and nobody sweeps the floor, because they might be driving good luck out of the house and into the yard. This is how the New Year starts, and in the various schools of astrology, including the simplified one described in this book, the Earthly Branch character cycle begins here as well.

Finally, the Earthly Branches designate a large cycle of twelve years over which the yin and yang balance one another out in the same pattern as in the day or the individual year. This cycle is also known by the names of Twelve Animals, each selected as representing the yin-yang characteristics of its associated Earthly Branch. Like the Earthly Branch characters, the animals have acquired their own distinct and rather human personalities, derived partly from folk mythology and literary association and partly from serious zoological observation. These characteristics are inherited by individuals born in the year designated with the particular animal name: people born in the year of the Mouse (*zi*) are as clever as mice, those from the Year of the Ox (*chou*) as strong as oxen, and so forth. This cycle of animal years is what is usually meant when people refer to the Chinese zodiac. Knowing about it is the easiest path to understanding the psychological insights of Chinese astrology, which is why this book follows the tradition of using the animal years as an organizing principle.

THE LIFE-SPAN CYCLE

An ideal life span of sixty years—ancient people were very lucky to live so long, even when times were good—can be divided into five twelve-year cycles: a Wood cycle to the age of twelve, the time of physical and intellectual growth and flexibility; a Fire cycle to twenty-four, the time of greatest strength and strongest passion; an Earth cycle to thirty-six, when people settle down and try to establish themselves between the generations of their parents and children; a Metal cycle to forty-eight when they try to exercise economic and social dominance over others; and a Water cycle to sixty, when physical decline is compensated by the attainment of wisdom and serenity.

This sixty-year Great Cycle is built into the Chinese calendar by naming each year with a combination of one Heavenly Stem character and one Earthly Branch character, providing a unique term for each year until the sixtieth, after which the cycle begins again. Great Cycles of this century began in 1864, 1924, and 1984, as you can see in the CALENDRICAL CONVERSION CHART on pp. 30–45.

The Great Cycle is also applied to the counting of months over a five-year period, days over a period of about two months, and hours over five days, so that each 120-minute "hour" over the course of the whole sixty years has its own unique designation in the form of eight characters. The designation of your birth hour is your own personal Eight Characters (*bazi*), and implicit in it is a complete characterization of the potential for harmony and disharmony in the first sixty years of your life, in terms of yin-yang interactions and the channeling of the *qi* force as they apply to possible relationships, times, places, and activities.

Thus, if you consult a professional Chinese astrologer, rather than drawing up a complicated star chart, he or she will focus on these eight characters, which are perfectly sufficient to define your position within all the cosmic cycles and to tell you, not what your fate is, but how to make the most of it: what strengths you should be maximizing, what weaknesses you should be minimizing, what kinds of conflicts you are likely to run into and what cyclical times they are likely to occur, how to concentrate the *qi* to take advantage of times or places of good luck, and how to avoid harm from the times and places of bad luck.

AN INVITATION

Obviously, it is impossible for this or any book to give even bare sketches for all of the hundreds of thousands of Eight Character combinations; that is why professional astrologers are in business. What we have done, instead, is to concentrate on the basic cycles of twelve, especially the twelve animal years and lunar months, as a way of providing a generous taste of the insights of Chinese astrology.

This means that when you apply the descriptions given in this book to yourself or your friends, you will find some things that fit amazingly well, and others that may not quite hit the mark. Keep in mind that we have not provided a complete description. You might also enjoy experimenting with enriching the description on your own, adding ideas based on the elements of the Great Cycle as given in the CALENDRICAL CONVERSION CHART and the birth hour as described in the "Favorable Hours" section of the animal year chapters (to find out where to look, match the hour to the animal in the circular chart below; e.g., for someone born at 11:30 at night, the relevant hour is between 11:00 PM and 1:00 AM, described in the chapter on the Year of the Mouse). Above all, have a good time, and don't take it too seriously! Remember that Chinese astrology does not offer you any kind of scientific "truth", but only a way of thinking about the truths you already know.

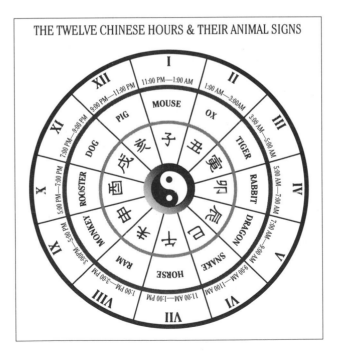

THE TWELVE CHINESE HOURS & THEIR ANIMAL SIGNS

CALENDRICAL
CONVERSION
CHART

This chart enables you to find the Animal Year, Element in the sixty-year cycle, and lunar month for any Western-calendar date from January 31, 1900, to early February of 2051. Although primarily intended to aid you in locating your date of birth according to the Chinese system, this chart also provides a handy 150-year guide to the commencement of the Chinese New Year, which falls on on the first day of the first lunar month, or moon, of each year.

The dates in the cells are the Western-calendar equivalents of the first day of each lunar month or moon; cells marked with an asterisk (*) indicate that this month is followed by an intercalary or "leap" month; e.g., the Eighth Moon of the Mouse year 1900, beginning on August 25, is followed by a second, intercalary Eighth Moon going on until October 22. To locate your birth moon, simply look for the two dates on the chart between which your birthday falls—your lunar month will be the one in which the the earlier of the two dates is listed. Here are four examples of how this system works:

MARCH 3, 1903. This comes between the first day of the Second Moon (February 27) of the Wood Rabbit Year 1903 and the first day of the Third Moon (March 29)—thus it is in the Second Moon of that year (the fifth day, to be precise).

JANUARY 6, 1903. The Wood Rabbit Year 1903 does not begin until January 29, the New Year's Day for that year, so someone born on January 6 is born in the previous Wood Tiger Year, labeled 1902, in the Twelfth Moon (i.e. after December 30).

JANUARY 3, 1902. In this case the person is born in the Eleventh Moon (between December 11, 1901 and January 10, 1902) of the Earth Ox Year labeled 1901.

JULY 22, 1903. Although this date is 52 days after the start of the Fifth Moon of the Wood Rabbit Year 1903, it is still considered as being in the Fifth Moon, namely the "leap" Fifth Moon of this year as indicated by the asterisk.

Solar Year	Element	Animal	1st Moon	2nd Moon	3rd Moon	4th Moon
1900	Water	Mouse	1/31	3/1	3/31	4/29
1901	Earth	Ox	2/19	3/20	4/19	5/18
1902	Wood	Tiger	2/8	3/10	4/8	5/8
1903	Wood	Rabbit	1/29	2/27	3/29	4/27
1904	Earth	Dragon	2/16	3/17	4/16	5/15
1905	Fire	Snake	2/4	3/6	4/5	5/4
1906	Fire	Horse	1/25	2/23	3/25	4/24*
1907	Earth	Ram	2/13	3/14	4/13	5/12
1908	Metal	Monkey	2/2	3/3	4/1	4/30
1909	Metal	Rooster	1/22	2/20*	4/20	5/19
1910	Earth	Dog	2/10	3/11	4/10	5/9
1911	Water	Pig	1/30	3/1	3/30	4/29
1912	Water	Mouse	2/18	3/19	4/17	5/17
1913	Earth	Ox	2/6	3/8	4/7	5/6
1914	Wood	Tiger	1/26	2/25	3/27	4/25
1915	Wood	Rabbit	2/14	3/16	4/14	5/14
1916	Earth	Dragon	2/4	3/4	4/3	5/2
1917	Fire	Snake	1/23	2/22	3/23*	5/21
1918	Fire	Horse	2/11	3/13	4/11	5/10
1919	Earth	Ram	2/1	3/2	4/1	4/30

Chinese New Year falls on the first day of the First Moon.

CALENDRICAL CONVERSION CHART

5TH MOON	6TH MOON	7TH MOON	8TH MOON	9TH MOON	10TH MOON	11TH MOON	12TH MOON
5/28	6/27	7/26	8/25*	10/23	11/22	12/22	1/20/01
6/16	7/16	8/14	9/13	10/12	11/11	12/11	1/10/02
6/6	7/5	8/4	9/2	10/2	10/31	11/30	12/30
5/27*	7/24	8/23	9/21	10/20	11/19	12/19	1/17/04
6/14	7/13	8/11	9/10	10/9	11/7	12/7	1/6/05
6/3	7/3	8/1	8/30	9/29	10/28	11/27	12/26
6/22	7/21	8/20	9/18	10/18	11/16	12/16	1/14/07
6/11	7/10	8/9	9/8	10/7	11/6	12/5	1/4/08
5/30	6/29	7/28	8/27	9/25	10/25	11/24	12/23
6/18	7/17	8/16	9/14	10/14	11/13	12/13	1/11/10
6/7	7/7	8/5	9/4	10/3	11/2	12/2	1/1/11
5/28	6/26*	8/24	9/22	10/22	11/21	12/20	1/19/12
6/15	7/14	8/13	9/11	10/10	11/9	12/9	1/7/13
6/5	7/4	8/2	9/1	9/30	10/29	11/28	12/27
5/25*	7/23	8/21	9/20	10/19	11/17	12/17	1/15/15
6/13	7/12	8/11	9/9	10/9	11/7	12/7	1/5/16
6/1	6/30	7/30	8/29	9/27	10/27	11/25	12/25
6/19	7/19	8/18	9/16	10/16	11/15	12/14	1/13/18
6/9	7/8	8/7	9/5	10/5	11/4	12/3	1/2/19
5/29	6/28	7/27*	9/24	10/24	11/22	12/22	1/21/20

*Indicates "leap moon."

Solar Year	Element	Animal	1st Moon	2nd Moon	3rd Moon	4th Moon
1920	Metal	Monkey	2/20	3/20	4/19	5/18
1921	Metal	Rooster	2/8	3/10	4/8	5/8
1922	Earth	Dog	1/28	2/27	3/28	4/27
1923	Water	Pig	2/16	3/17	4/16	5/16
1924	Water	Mouse	2/5	3/5	4/4	5/4
1925	Earth	Ox	1/24	2/23	3/24	4/23*
1926	Wood	Tiger	2/13	3/14	4/12	5/12
1927	Wood	Rabbit	2/2	3/4	4/2	5/1
1928	Earth	Dragon	1/23	2/21*	4/20	5/19
1929	Fire	Snake	2/10	3/11	4/10	5/9
1930	Fire	Horse	1/30	2/28	3/30	4/29
1931	Earth	Ram	2/17	3/19	4/18	5/17
1932	Metal	Monkey	2/6	3/7	4/6	5/6
1933	Metal	Rooster	1/26	2/24	3/26	4/25
1934	Earth	Dog	2/14	3/15	4/14	5/13
1935	Water	Pig	2/4	3/5	4/3	5/3
1936	Water	Mouse	1/24	2/23	3/23*	5/21
1937	Earth	Ox	2/11	3/13	4/11	5/10
1938	Wood	Tiger	1/31	3/2	4/1	4/30
1939	Wood	Rabbit	2/19	3/21	4/20	5/19

Chinese New Year falls on the first day of the First Moon.

5TH MOON	6TH MOON	7TH MOON	8TH MOON	9TH MOON	10TH MOON	11TH MOON	12TH MOON
6/16	7/16	8/14	9/12	10/12	11/10	12/10	1/9/21
6/6	7/5	8/4	9/2	10/1	10/31	11/29	12/29
5/27*	7/24	8/23	9/21	10/20	11/19	12/18	1/17/23
6/14	7/14	8/12	9/11	10/10	11/8	12/8	1/6/24
6/2	7/2	8/1	8/30	9/29	10/28	11/27	12/26
6/21	7/21	8/19	9/18	10/18	11/16	12/16	1/14/26
6/10	7/10	8/8	9/7	10/7	11/5	12/5	1/4/27
5/31	6/29	7/29	8/27	9/26	10/25	11/24	12/24
6/18	7/17	8/15	9/14	10/13	11/12	12/12	1/11/29
6/7	7/7	8/5	9/3	10/3	11/1	12/1	12/31
5/28	6/26*	8/24	9/22	10/22	11/20	12/20	1/19/31
6/16	7/15	8/14	9/12	10/11	11/10	12/9	1/8/32
6/4	7/4	8/2	9/1	9/30	10/29	11/28	12/27
5/24*	7/23	8/21	9/20	10/19	11/18	12/17	1/15/34
6/12	7/12	8/10	9/9	10/8	11/7	12/7	1/5/35
6/1	7/1	7/30	8/29	9/28	10/27	11/26	12/26
6/19	7/18	8/17	9/16	10/15	11/14	12/14	1/13/37
6/9	7/8	8/6	9/5	10/4	11/3	12/3	1/2/38
5/29	6/28	7/27*	9/24	10/23	11/22	12/22	1/20/39
6/17	7/17	8/15	9/13	10/13	11/11	12/11	1/9/40

*Indicates "leap moon."

Solar Year	Element	Animal	1st Moon	2nd Moon	3rd Moon	4th Moon
1940	Earth	Dragon	2/8	3/9	4/8	5/7
1941	Fire	Snake	1/27	2/26	3/28	4/26
1942	Fire	Horse	2/15	3/17	4/15	5/15
1943	Earth	Ram	2/5	3/6	4/5	5/4
1944	Metal	Monkey	1/25	2/24	3/24	4/23*
1945	Metal	Rooster	2/13	3/14	4/12	5/12
1946	Earth	Dog	2/2	3/4	4/2	5/1
1947	Water	Pig	1/22	2/21*	4/21	5/20
1948	Water	Mouse	2/10	3/11	4/9	5/9
1949	Earth	Ox	1/29	2/28	3/29	4/28
1950	Wood	Tiger	2/17	3/18	4/17	5/17
1951	Wood	Rabbit	2/6	3/8	4/6	5/6
1952	Earth	Dragon	1/27	2/25	3/26	4/24
1953	Fire	Snake	2/14	3/15	4/14	5/13
1954	Fire	Horse	2/3	3/5	4/3	5/3
1955	Earth	Ram	1/24	2/22	3/24*	5/22
1956	Metal	Monkey	2/12	3/12	4/11	5/10
1957	Metal	Rooster	1/31	3/2	3/31	4/30
1958	Earth	Dog	2/18	3/20	4/19	5/19
1959	Water	Pig	2/8	3/9	4/8	5/8

Chinese New Year falls on the first day of the First Moon.

CALENDRICAL CONVERSION CHART

5TH MOON	6TH MOON	7TH MOON	8TH MOON	9TH MOON	10TH MOON	11TH MOON	12TH MOON
6/6	7/5	8/4	9/2	10/1	10/31	11/29	12/29
5/26	6/25*	8/23	9/21	10/20	11/19	12/18	1/17/42
6/14	7/13	8/12	9/10	10/10	11/8	12/8	1/6/43
6/3	7/2	8/1	8/31	9/29	10/29	11/27	12/27
6/21	7/20	8/19	9/17	10/17	11/16	12/15	1/14/45
6/10	7/9	8/8	9/6	10/6	11/5	12/5	1/3/46
5/31	6/29	7/28	8/27	9/25	10/25	11/24	12/23
6/19	7/18	8/16	9/15	10/14	11/13	12/12	1/11/48
6/7	7/7	8/5	9/3	10/3	11/1	12/1	12/30
5/28	6/26	7/26*	9/22	10/22	11/20	12/20	1/18/50
6/15	7/15	8/14	9/12	10/11	11/10	12/9	1/8/51
6/5	7/4	8/3	9/1	10/1	10/30	11/29	12/28
5/24*	7/22	8/20	9/19	10/19	11/17	12/17	1/15/54
6/11	7/11	8/10	9/8	10/8	11/7	12/6	1/5/54
6/1	6/30	7/30	8/28	9/27	10/27	11/25	12/25
6/20	7/19	8/18	9/16	10/16	11/14	12/14	1/13/56
6/9	7/8	8/6	9/5	10/4	11/3	12/2	1/1/57
5/29	6/28	7/27	8/25*	10/23	11/22	12/21	1/20/58
6/17	7/17	8/15	9/13	10/13	11/11	12/11	1/9/59
6/6	7/6	8/4	9/3	10/2	11/1	11/30	12/30

*Indicates "leap moon."

SOLAR YEAR	ELEMENT	ANIMAL	1ST MOON	2ND MOON	3RD MOON	4TH MOON
1960	Water	Mouse	1/28	2/27	3/27	4/26
1961	Earth	Ox	2/15	3/17	4/15	5/15
1962	Wood	Tiger	2/5	3/6	4/5	5/4
1963	Wood	Rabbit	1/25	2/24	3/25	4/24*
1964	Earth	Dragon	2/13	3/14	4/12	5/12
1965	Fire	Snake	2/2	3/3	4/2	5/1
1966	Fire	Horse	1/21	2/20	3/22*	5/20
1967	Earth	Ram	2/9	3/11	4/10	5/9
1968	Metal	Monkey	1/30	2/28	3/29	4/27
1969	Metal	Rooster	2/17	3/18	4/17	5/16
1970	Earth	Dog	2/6	3/8	4/6	5/5
1971	Water	Pig	1/27	2/25	3/27	4/25
1972	Water	Mouse	2/15	3/15	4/14	5/13
1973	Earth	Ox	2/3	3/5	4/3	5/3
1974	Wood	Tiger	1/23	2/22	3/24	4/22*
1975	Wood	Rabbit	2/11	3/13	4/12	5/11
1976	Earth	Dragon	1/31	3/1	3/31	4/29
1977	Fire	Snake	2/18	3/20	4/18	5/18
1978	Fire	Horse	2/7	3/9	4/7	5/7
1979	Earth	Ram	1/28	2/27	3/28	4/26

Chinese New Year falls on the first day of the First Moon.

CALENDRICAL CONVERSION CHART

5TH MOON	6TH MOON	7TH MOON	8TH MOON	9TH MOON	10TH MOON	11TH MOON	12TH MOON
5/25	6/24*	8/22	9/21	10/20	11/19	12/18	1/17/61
6/13	7/13	8/11	9/10	10/10	11/8	12/8	1/6/62
6/2	7/2	7/31	8/30	9/29	10/28	11/27	12/27
6/21	7/21	8/19	9/18	10/17	11/16	12/16	1/15/64
6/10	7/9	8/8	9/6	10/6	11/4	12/4	1/3/65
5/31	6/29	7/28	8/27	9/25	10/24	11/23	12/23
6/19	7/18	8/16	9/15	10/14	11/12	12/12	1/11/67
6/8	7/8	8/6	9/4	10/4	11/2	12/2	12/31
5/27	6/26	7/25*	9/22	10/22	11/20	12/20	1/18/69
6/15	7/14	8/13	9/12	10/11	11/10	12/9	1/8/70
6/4	7/3	8/2	9/1	9/30	10/30	11/29	12/28
5/24*	7/22	8/21	9/19	10/19	11/18	12/18	1/16/72
6/11	7/11	8/9	9/8	10/7	11/6	12/6	1/4/73
6/1	6/30	7/30	8/28	9/26	10/26	11/25	12/24
6/20	7/19	8/18	9/16	10/15	11/14	12/14	1/12/75
6/10	7/9	8/7	9/6	10/5	11/3	12/3	1/1/76
5/29	6/27	7/27	8/25*	10/23	11/21	12/21	1/19/77
6/17	7/16	8/15	9/13	10/13	11/11	12/11	1/9/78
6/6	7/5	8/4	9/3	10/2	11/1	11/30	12/30
5/26	6/24*	8/23	9/21	10/21	11/20	12/19	1/18/80

*Indicates "leap moon."

37

Solar Year	Element	Animal	1st Moon	2nd Moon	3rd Moon	4th Moon
1980	Metal	Monkey	2/16	3/17	4/15	5/14
1981	Metal	Rooster	2/5	3/6	4/5	5/4
1982	Earth	Dog	1/25	2/24	3/25	4/24*
1983	Water	Pig	2/13	3/15	4/13	5/13
1984	Water	Mouse	2/2	3/3	4/1	5/1
1985	Earth	Ox	2/20	3/21	4/20	5/20
1986	Wood	Tiger	2/9	3/10	4/9	5/9
1987	Wood	Rabbit	1/29	2/28	3/29	4/28
1988	Earth	Dragon	2/17	3/18	4/16	5/16
1989	Fire	Snake	2/6	3/8	4/6	5/5
1990	Fire	Horse	1/27	2/25	3/27	4/25
1991	Earth	Ram	2/15	3/16	4/15	5/14
1992	Metal	Monkey	2/4	3/4	4/3	5/3
1993	Metal	Rooster	1/23	2/21	3/23*	5/21
1994	Earth	Dog	2/10	3/12	4/11	5/11
1995	Water	Pig	1/31	3/1	3/31	4/30
1996	Water	Mouse	2/19	3/19	4/18	5/17
1997	Earth	Ox	2/7	3/9	4/7	5/7
1998	Wood	Tiger	1/28	2/27	3/28	4/26
1999	Wood	Rabbit	2/16	3/18	4/16	5/15

Chinese New Year falls on the first day of the First Moon.

CALENDRICAL CONVERSION CHART

5TH MOON	6TH MOON	7TH MOON	8TH MOON	9TH MOON	10TH MOON	11TH MOON	12TH MOON
6/13	7/12	8/11	9/9	10/9	11/8	12/7	1/6/81
6/2	7/2	7/31	8/29	9/28	10/28	11/26	12/26
6/21	7/21	8/19	9/17	10/17	11/15	12/15	1/14/83
6/11	7/10	8/9	9/7	10/6	11/5	12/4	1/3/84
5/31	6/29	7/28	8/27	9/25	10/24*	12/22	1/21/85
6/18	7/18	8/16	9/15	10/14	11/12	12/12	1/10/86
6/7	7/7	8/6	9/4	10/4	11/2	12/2	12/31
5/27	6/26*	8/24	9/23	10/23	11/21	12/21	1/19/88
6/14	7/14	8/12	9/11	10/11	11/9	12/9	1/8/89
6/4	7/3	8/2	8/31	9/30	10/29	11/28	12/28
5/24*	7/22	8/20	9/19	10/18	11/17	12/17	1/16/91
6/12	7/12	8/10	9/8	10/8	11/6	12/6	1/5/92
6/1	6/30	7/30	8/28	9/26	10/26	11/24	12/24
6/20	7/19	8/18	9/16	10/15	11/14	12/13	1/12/94
6/9	7/9	8/7	9/6	10/5	11/3	12/3	1/1/95
5/29	6/28	7/27	8/26*	10/24	11/22	12/22	1/20/96
6/16	7/16	8/14	9/13	10/12	11/11	12/11	1/9/97
6/5	7/5	8/3	9/2	10/2	10/31	11/30	12/30
5/26*	7/23	8/22	9/21	10/20	11/19	12/19	1/17/99
6/14	7/13	8/11	9/10	10/9	11/8	12/8	1/7/00

*Indicates "leap moon."

SOLAR YEAR	ELEMENT	ANIMAL	1ST MOON	2ND MOON	3RD MOON	4TH MOON
2000	Earth	Dragon	2/5	3/6	4/5	5/4
2001	Fire	Snake	1/24	2/23	3/25	4/23*
2002	Fire	Horse	2/12	3/14	4/13	5/12
2003	Earth	Ram	2/1	3/3	4/2	5/1
2004	Metal	Monkey	1/22	2/20*	4/19	5/19
2005	Metal	Rooster	2/9	3/10	4/9	5/8
2006	Earth	Dog	1/29	2/28	3/29	4/28
2007	Water	Pig	2/18	3/19	4/17	5/17
2008	Water	Mouse	2/7	3/8	4/6	5/5
2009	Earth	Ox	1/26	2/25	3/27	4/25
2010	Wood	Tiger	2/14	3/16	4/14	5/14
2011	Wood	Rabbit	2/3	3/5	4/3	5/3
2012	Earth	Dragon	1/23	2/22	3/22	4/21*
2013	Fire	Snake	2/10	3/12	4/10	5/10
2014	Fire	Horse	1/31	3/1	3/31	4/29
2015	Earth	Ram	2/19	3/20	4/19	5/18
2016	Metal	Monkey	2/8/	3/9	4/7	5/7
2017	Metal	Rooster	1/28	2/26	3/28	4/26
2018	Earth	Dog	2/16	3/17	4/16	5/15
2019	Water	Pig	2/5	3/6	4/5	5/5

Chinese New Year falls on the first day of the First Moon.

CALENDRICAL CONVERSION CHART

5TH MOON	6TH MOON	7TH MOON	8TH MOON	9TH MOON	10TH MOON	11TH MOON	12TH MOON
6/2	7/2	7/31	8/29	9/28	10/27	11/26	12/26
6/21	7/21	8/19	9/17	10/17	11/15	12/15	1/13/02
6/11	7/10	8/9	9/7	10/6	11/5	12/4	1/3/03
5/31	6/30	7/29	8/28	9/26	10/25	11/24	12/23
6/18	7/17	8/16	9/14	10/14	11/12	12/12	1/10/05
6/7	7/6	8/5	9/4	10/3	11/2	12/1	12/31
5/27	6/26	7/25*	9/22	10/22	11/21	12/20	1/19/07
6/15	7/14	8/13	9/11	10/11	11/10	12/10	1/8/08
6/4	7/3	8/1	8/31	9/29	10/29	11/28	12/27
5/24*	7/22	8/20	9/19	10/18	11/17	12/16	1/15/10
6/12	7/12	8/10	9/8	10/8	11/6	12/6	1/4/11
6/2	7/1	7/31	8/29	9/27	10/27	11/25	12/25
6/19	7/19	8/17	9/16	10/15	11/14	12/13	1/12/13
6/9	7/8	8/7	9/5	10/5	11/3	12/3	1/1/14
5/29	6/27	7/27	8/25	9/24*	11/22	12/22	1/20/15
6/16	7/16	8/14	9/13	10/13	11/12	12/11	1/10/16
6/5	7/4	8/3	9/1	10/1	10/31	11/29	12/29
5/26	6/24*	8/22	9/20	10/20	11/18	12/18	1/17/18
6/14	7/13	8/11	9/10	10/9	11/8	12/7	1/6/19
6/3	7/3	8/1	8/30	9/29	10/28	11/26	12/26

*Indicates "leap moon."

41

Solar Year	Element	Animal	1st Moon	2nd Moon	3rd Moon	4th Moon
2020	Water	Mouse	1/25	2/23	3/24	4/23*
2021	Earth	Ox	2/12	3/13	4/12	5/12
2022	Wood	Tiger	2/1	3/3	4/1	5/1
2023	Wood	Rabbit	1/22	2/20*	4/20	5/19
2024	Earth	Dragon	2/10	3/10	4/9	5/8
2025	Fire	Snake	1/29	2/28	3/29	4/28
2026	Fire	Horse	2/17	3/19	4/16	5/17
2027	Earth	Ram	2/6	3/8	4/7	5/6
2028	Metal	Monkey	1/26	2/24	3/26	4/25
2029	Metal	Rooster	2/13	3/15	4/14	5/13
2030	Earth	Dog	2/3	3/4	4/3	5/2
2031	Water	Pig	1/23	2/21	3/23*	5/21
2032	Water	Mouse	2/11	3/12	4/10	5/9
2033	Earth	Ox	1/31	3/1	3/31	4/29
2034	Wood	Tiger	2/19	3/20	4/19	5/18
2035	Wood	Rabbit	2/8	3/10	4/8	5/8
2036	Earth	Dragon	1/28	2/26	3/28	4/26
2037	Fire	Snake	2/15	3/17	4/16	5/15
2038	Fire	Horse	2/4	3/6	4/5	5/4
2039	Earth	Ram	1/24	2/23	3/25	4/23

Chinese New Year falls on the first day of the First Moon.

CALENDRICAL CONVERSION CHART

5TH MOON	6TH MOON	7TH MOON	8TH MOON	9TH MOON	10TH MOON	11TH MOON	12TH MOON
6/21	7/21	8/19	9/17	10/17	11/15	12/15	1/13/21
6/10	7/10	8/8	9/7	10/6	11/5	12/4	1/3/22
5/28	6/29	7/29	8/27	9/26	10/25	11/24	12/23
6/18	7/18	8/15	9/15	10/14	11/13	12/13	1/11/24
6/6	7/6	8/4	9/3	10/3	11/1	12/1	12/31
5/25	6/25*	8/23	9/22	10/21	11/20	12/20	1/19/26
6/15	7/14	8/13	9/11	10/10	11/10	12/9	1/8/27
6/5	7/4	8/2	9/1	9/30	10/29	11/28	12/28
5/24*	7/22	8/20	9/19	10/18	11/16	12/16	1/15/29
6/12	7/11	8/10	9/8	10/8	11/6	12/5	1/4/30
6/1	7/1	7/30	8/29	9/27	10/27	11/25	12/25
6/20	7/19	8/18	9/17	10/16	11/15	12/14	1/13/32
6/8	7/7	8/6	9/5	10/4	11/3	12/3	1/1/33
5/28	6/27	7/26*	9/23	10/23	11/22	12/22	1/20/34
6/16	7/16	8/14	9/13	10/12	11/11	12/11	1/9/35
6/6	7/5	8/4	9/2	10/1	10/31	11/30	12/29
5/26	6/24*	8/22	9/20	10/19	11/18	12/17	1/16/37
6/14	7/13	8/11	9/10	10/9	11/7	12/7	1/5/38
6/3	7/2	8/1	8/30	9/29	10/28	11/26	12/26
5/23*	7/21	8/20	9/18	10/18	11/16	12/16	1/14/40

*Indicates "leap moon."

Solar Year	Element	Animal	1st Moon	2nd Moon	3rd Moon	4th Moon
2040	Metal	Monkey	2/12	3/13	4/11	5/11
2041	Metal	Rooster	2/1	3/2	4/1	4/30
2042	Earth	Dog	1/22	2/20*	4/20	5/19
2043	Water	Pig	2/10	3/11	4/10	5/9
2044	Water	Mouse	1/30	2/28	3/29	4/28
2045	Earth	Ox	2/17	3/19	4/17	5/17
2046	Wood	Tiger	2/6	3/8	4/6	5/6
2047	Wood	Rabbit	1/26	2/25	3/26	4/25
2048	Earth	Dragon	2/14	3/14	4/13	5/13
2049	Fire	Snake	2/2	3/4	4/2	5/2
2050	Fire	Horse	1/23	2/21	3/23*	5/21

Chinese New Year falls on the first day of the First Moon.

CALENDRICAL CONVERSION CHART

5TH MOON	6TH MOON	7TH MOON	8TH MOON	9TH MOON	10TH MOON	11TH MOON	12TH MOON
6/10	7/9	8/8	9/6	10/6	11/5	12/4	1/3/41
5/31	6/28	7/28	8/27	9/25	10/25	11/24	12/23
6/18	7/17	8/16	9/14	10/14	11/13	12/12	1/11/43
6/7	7/7	8/5	9/3	10/3	11/2	12/1	12/31
5/27	6/25	7/25*	9/21	10/21	11/19	12/19	1/18/45
6/15	7/14	8/13	9/11	10/10	11/9	12/8	1/7/46
6/4	7/4	8/2	9/1	9/30	10/29	11/28	12/27
5/25*	7/23	8/21	9/20	10/19	11/17	12/17	1/15/48
6/11	7/11	8/10	9/8	10/8	11/6	12/5	1/4/49
5/31	6/30	7/30	8/28	9/27	10/27	11/25	12/25
6/19	7/19	8/17	9/16	10/16	11/14	12/14	1/13/51

*Indicates "leap moon."

THE
CHINESE
ZODIAC

THE YEAR
OF THE
MOUSE

ZI

MOUSE YEARS

1900	January 31 to February 18, 1901
1912	February 18 to February 5, 1913
1924	February 5 to January 23, 1925
1936	January 24 to February 10, 1937
1948	February 10 to January 28, 1949
1960	January 28 to February 14, 1961
1972	February 15 to February 2, 1973
1984	February 2 to February 19, 1985
1996	February 19 to February 6, 1997
2008	February 7 to January 25, 2009
2020	January 25 to February 11, 2021
2032	February 11 to January 30, 2033
2044	January 30 to February 16, 2045

ASSOCIATIONS

EARTHLY BRANCH CHARACTER: *Zi* is a picture of a newborn infant, with its arms sticking out of its swaddling clothes, and denotes a child, or a seed; this character is associated with posterity, and by extension continuity. Just as the full-grown plant is mysteriously concealed within the seed, or the adult in the child, so the essence of those born in the Year of the Mouse is concealment. Mouse people play their cards very close to the chest, letting their grand plans ripen even as they appear to be running around town having a good time, up to nothing in particular. Their good qualities are youthful ones: they are optimistic, creative, and witty.

ANIMAL: In Chinese mythology, mice and rats are considered very wise creatures, with arcane or even occult knowledge. According to one folk belief, a rat lives to the age of three hundred, and when it reaches one hundred its color changes to white and it acquires the gift of prophecy.

The mouse *(shu)* is nervous and analytical, always curious, and bold enough to take risks, but at the same time makes use of its intelligence to weigh the risk factors carefully and avoid dangers and traps. It is also secretive and sexy. Mouse people may be said to take a more intellectual than physical approach to life, but they don't care to be seen working things out. They also have a great appetite for pleasure, loving night life and all the other good things life has to offer. They find it hard to give in their emotional lives, but are generous with material things.

ORDER: The first position in the Chinese zodiac is above all a position of respect; and mouse people are capable of rising to the highest positions of leadership in all fields, if they can maintain a balanced harmony with their environment in life and work. Respect must be earned, of course, and not thrown away out of an excessive desire for privacy manifesting itself as false modesty.

ELEMENT: Water, which is in harmony with Wood and Metal, but in conflict with Fire. The Water element connotes nourishment, and mouse people express themselves best in areas related to food, fertility, children, and land. More generally, they draw strength from the well of their own hidden resources. Their weakness is in depending too much on themselves, causing terrible internal stress, instead of using their considerable social skills to gain support from others.

STAR GROUP: The Palace of the Year of the Mouse is ruled by the Earth Star (Saturn), and it houses four very important Lodges: Dou, Niu, Nu, and Xu, corresponding to the stars within the Western constellations of Sagittarius, Aries, Aquarius, and Equuleus. Those who follow Chinese astrology in depth warn against the danger of major conflict with those born in the Year of the Horse. On a more general level, conflict arises from the contradictions of the divided self of people born in the Year of the Mouse—between the happy-go-lucky outside and the anxiety-ridden, plotting inside—which may make more straightforward creatures doubt their sincerity. Mostly, however, their intelligence and generosity earn them respect and support.

FAVORABLE DIRECTION: North is the favored direction for projects and voyages of those born in the Year of the Mouse. It is also the most auspicious point of all on the Chinese compass, as the site of the constellation known in the West as the Great Bear or Big Dipper . In Chinese mythology, North is the home of the Dark Warrior Wu Chang and his two attendants, a turtle and a snake, whose eternal struggle with one another is the source of Wu Chang's balance and wisdom. Wu Chang is also the god of the sea and the protector of seamen, since the North Star in the Big Dipper provides them with a beacon for a safe voyage home.

The Dark Warrior's domain is winter. He is associated with the element of Water, and the power of floods, frosts, and snow. People born in the Year of the Mouse will do well to orient their projects and homes toward the north; traveling in

China, they will enjoy above all sightseeing—and eating—in the capital of Beijing.

FAVORABLE MONTH: Late January to mid or late February, the post-harvest months when the storehouses are stocked with food and wine, and mice are happy and active, enjoying the fruits of efforts expended in the previous year. Mouse people should also take care at this time to think about their plans, projects, and goals for continued success. In China, this is the first lunar month, the time of year when feasting and celebration never seem to end.

FAVORABLE HOUR: 11:00 PM to 1:00 AM, the midnight hour when the dark yin force reaches its zenith. Despite the mouse's love for parties and going out, this should not be a time for wild activities but for getting away from it all and into one's own private world. It is a time for rest, recharging, and preparing the next step, not only to ensure success, but also for protection and self-preservation.

FAVORABLE NUMBERS: 1, 4, 5, 10, 14, 41, 45, 51, 54.

THE WHOLE PERSON

CHARACTER: Those born in the Year of the Mouse are curious, witty, and creative, fast talkers and high livers, who take a more intellectual than physical approach to life but nevertheless passionately enjoy all its material pleasures. They are risk-takers, but usually calculate the risks precisely before leaping into action. They are discreet and often even secretive about what is on their minds, but at the same time value companionship more than anything else. Their generous helping hand is always available to friends and lovers.

After sundown, when the evening candles are lit, you see mouse people at their liveliest. It is not good for them to hide in their nests munching on snacks and drinking rice-wine by themselves; later in the evening, though, they will have to make time to be alone. Their wit, creativity, and curiosity make them good critics with keen, deep insight, and their advice and insight are well-respected by friends and enemies alike.

EMOTIONS: While mouse people outwardly maintain their composure with a look of calm, maturity, and charm, this is partly because of their natural discretion. Internally they tend to be emotional, subject to inner stress and quiet discontent behind the facade. When alone they go through endless bouts of anxiety, restlessness, nervousness, and bad temper; even in the middle of a group activity they are likely to retire to a private corner to do their own thinking.

Intensely romantic and intensely social at the same time, outside their necessary private moments they need constant companionship and love, and this makes them sensitive, sentimental, and vulnerable. It is through these qualities that the mouse person can be opened to deeper emotional dimensions.

WEAKNESSES: Mouse people can be opportunistic, excessively aggressive, and quietly manipulative. Their love of gambling, combined with obsessive weighing of all the risks, often leaves them suffering from a gnawing fear of failure and from sleepless nights. Of course the same characteristics are the typical ingredients of mouse success, as they manipulate their way with smooth talk and creative planning.

LIFESTYLE: Mouse people love life, especially social life in the nighttime. They are fond of fun, shopping, and all kinds of tasty foods: dim sum, noodles, sweets and baked goods, fine teas and wines. They revel in touches of luxury and comfort: fine cars, fine restaurants, dance and music, as well as very serious collections of antiques, books, stamps, and so on.

FAMOUS MOUSE PEOPLE: Louis Armstrong, Irving Berlin, Constantin Brancusi, Marlon Brando, Truman Capote, Antonio Gaudí, Galileo Galilei, Joseph Haydn, Margaret Mitchell, Claude Monet, Louise Nevelson, Eugene O'Neill, Jackson Pollack, Auguste Rodin, Johann Strauss, William Shakespeare, Petr

Il'ich Tchaikovsky, Lev Tolstoi, Jules Verne, Frank Winfield Woolworth, George Washington.

MOUSE PEOPLE BORN IN THE...

Note: Western-calendar months are given as approximations only; to find a birth moon according to the Chinese lunisolar calendar, consult the chart on pp. 30–45.

FIRST MOON (FEBRUARY): Mouse people born in this moon are sensitive and instinctive but restless. They have a tendency to overstep themselves without realizing what they are getting themselves into; happily, they are also skilled at turning a bad situation to their favor. Their creative abilities are well suited to setting new trends and fashions. They are controversial, dramatic, and usually attractive, with delicate skin and features.

SECOND MOON (MARCH): These mouse people are quiet thinkers and planners, intellectual and analytical, and at the same time skeptical and witty. They are completely indifferent to many things, and although they are friendly and hard-working, it is not easy to understand them or to figure out what they are plotting after. They enjoy privacy more than others. They make insightful researchers, creative artists, critics, and financial planners.

THIRD MOON (APRIL): Less cautious as gamblers than others born in this year, they love to go against the odds, and are often very lucky, favored by the youthful yang force of this month. Their restlessness, however, torments them most of their lives; no success ever seems enough, until they finally reach a late maturity and inner peace.

FOURTH MOON (MAY): Reserved and cautious, they are very practical in getting what they want in life. These are successful people in whatever they do, and precisely because of this they must be careful in their selection of activities, since they are equally open to the good and the bad.

FIFTH MOON (JUNE): Highly artistic and emotionally deep. Sometimes very intense and obsessive, they need to be constantly reminded that the objective view may be in contrast with their own. If they master harmony and balance, they can unite their contradictions into something bigger than either side. As creative persons they enjoy a good sense of design and order. They tend to be very body-oriented, especially with regard to cleanliness and organization.

SIXTH MOON (JULY): Happy mouse people who love all the good things in life: beautiful presentation, shopping and spending money, dining, parties and games, and colorful events. They are social, talkative, witty, and calculating, aiming at drawing attention to themselves for personal gain. Making waves and generating excitement, they make excellent salespeople and politicians.

SEVENTH MOON (AUGUST): The yang energy of this month is too strong to submit to the yin of the mouse year. Creative, insecure, and emotional, they may act calm and mature but their internal struggles are severe. They are often unhappy, lonely, and susceptible to mood swings; on the other hand these emotions open them up to deeper creative forces and ideas. It may be wise for them to find protection with more secure mates, or wait for their careers to be established before they marry.

EIGHTH MOON (SEPTEMBER): Very capable people who are quick, alert, intelligent, and artistic, they are usually lucky and successful in whatever they do. However, their confidence can easily lead them into heavy-handed grasping after power and authority. They are dramatic lovers, and quite possessive. Success at work may not translate to success in intimate personal matters; love will come when life has tamed them to some extent.

NINTH MOON (OCTOBER): Perfectionist thinkers and planners, they are both demanding of others and creative on their own. They can be highly critical, skeptical, clever, and witty. Agile, active, and restless, they are not easy to get close to and find it difficult to get close to others. They are great performers and achievers in work, but hard to live with.

TENTH MOON (NOVEMBER): Lucky people, with lots of good things going for them in life. Like children in a toy store, they are aggressive and calculating in getting what they want. Too many discontents and distractions can easily turn good things into bad, especially romance and love. Beware of addictions of any kind: alcohol, gambling, drugs, fast driving, etc.

ELEVENTH MOON (DECEMBER): Artistic and strong-minded people, intelligent and highly curious about everything, they are easily distracted or involved in too many things at the same time, causing losses in concentration and focus that they may later regret. Gentle balance and objectivity can provide a basis for tolerance and patience, leading to further success and new horizons. These mouse people are resourceful enough to find their own ways eventually.

TWELFTH MOON (JANUARY OF FOLLOWING YEAR): Sharing some influences with the coming Year of the Ox, their talkative nature masks a quiet stubbornness and aggression. They are persistent and calculating in getting things they want. Slow but hard-working, they have great reserves of energy for the achievement of long-term goals. At times their stubbornness can be insensitive and inconsiderate, creating situations that are difficult for others. Fortunately they are intelligent and friendly, smooth talkers who know their skills well.

THE LIFE CYCLE

HEALTH: There is a tendency for mouse people to worry constantly about their health, and not without reason, because they are vulnerable to all sorts of diseases and stress-related syndromes. As party people, they need to pay very careful attention to diet, especially overindulgence in fatty foods, smoking, drinking, and drugs. Silent and cumulative food-related health problems can be fatal.

MONEY: The two things mouse people are obsessive about and good at are sex and money. Their combination of bold and aggressive risk-taking behavior with a cautious, calculating, analytical nature makes them shrewd investors, excellent deal makers, and astute financial planners. Creativity and curiosity enable them to find ways to turn every step and procedure toward profit. They work best in projects associated with food, fertility, children, and land.

CAREER: The talent and intelligence of mouse people suit them for any kind of career. You will find them succeeding as accountants, businesspeople, critics, designers, financial planners, lawyers, engineers, dancers, artists, musicians, writers, medical professionals, scientists and technicians, entertainers, and politicians.

LOVE: Sex is an obsession and a talent with mouse people. They are not necessarily very good at fidelity, being warm, lovable, and desirable, and having many chances to meet mates at all the parties and social events they organize. After dark, song and music, dancing and intimate dinners ignite a seductive mood which keeps the love-fire burning until dawn.

Once truly in love, mouse people make hot and intense lovers, and love helps them overcome their innate emotional secretiveness, as a result of which they may expose themselves to hurt feelings and resentment against those who do not respond. They fight and cry with those they love, break up, and in the end compromise and return.

MOUSE PARTNERS BORN
IN THE YEAR OF THE...

MOUSE: Two mice together can entertain one another constantly, singing songs, going to the movies, sharing late suppers, and so on into the night, but they must restrain their mouse curiosity and respect one another's secrets. The negative side is that this may never be a deep relationship, but it is guaranteed to be fun.

OX: The mouse can derive many benefits from the stability and strength of the enduring ox person. What they have in common is a mutually reinforcing optimism that enables them to put aside their worries and enjoy a sunny day or moonlit night together. A long-lasting and happy relationship.

TIGER: Caution is advised when the mouse decides to hunt for a tiger: the mouse is liable to get its tail stepped on, and that could be painful! On the other hand, when the tiger condescends to hunt the mouse, it may be surprised by the mouse's strength. The odds against this conflicted relationship going anywhere are great, but if it does finally work out, both parties learn more than they ever expected.

RABBIT: The rabbit has a lot in common with the mouse, being every bit as clever, and even faster. Their relationship is too good to be true, and it usually isn't true: a nice fling, but not likely to last. As the mouse asks for more commitment, the rabbit asks for more freedom. Advisable only for the mouse that is not in a monogamous mood.

DRAGON: Sexually, there isn't any match better than this one, and mouse finds it quite addictive. The danger is that dragon may eventually tire of trying to find its way into mouse's secret core, and then go into one of its periodic transformations and fly away. Once the spell is broken it cannot be restored, and since this is the one partner that the mouse cannot bear to lose, caution is essential.

SNAKE: Mouse may think it shares lots of interests and common ground with this clever, quiet, and tricky mate, but it may be heading for trouble; the snake can swallow the mouse entirely and quietly any time it chooses. This is a *liaison dangereuse*, in typical cases less a romance than a hostile game of wits which the mouse is likely to lose. Still, it can be a valuable learning experience.

HORSE: Given the potential for conflict between the star groups of these two signs, the mouse and the horse are advised to steer clear of one another. They do feel each other's attraction, however, and may find it hard to resist. If so, they had better prepare for rough seas, and keep a life raft handy!

RAM: These two meet at museums and concerts, think they are speaking the same language, and find when they get home that there's nothing to say. They are not likely to be so attracted to one another that they will put out the effort to make it work. The active, satirical mouse is makes fun of the ram, and in the end hurts it. If mouse can't learn to be kind it had better break things off gently.

MONKEY: Mouse and monkey don't inhabit the same social worlds, on the whole, and rarely meet. When they do, they couldn't care less about common interests—they're in love! They can share the same tree: one above on the branches, the other underground near the roots. As long as the rules of the game are clearly established, they can work well together.

ROOSTER: The mouse comes out at night, stealing the chickens' feed and often their eggs as well. But it had better beware of venturing into the chicken-yard during the day, because its natural enemy, the rooster, is waiting for it. These two often enjoy working together, but a mouse that believes in a rooster's love is either naive or too clever by half.

DOG: Dog and mouse can easily be good friends, sharing the early part of the evening and visiting each other's homes, but it is not advisable for them to get too close. The dog won't leave the mouse any personal space and will tag along after it, worry it, and eventually nip at it. It will take a very tolerant mouse to put up with this, and a mouse that tolerant may get hurt.

PIG: The pig is very nice to the mouse, going along with all its wild ideas, yet leaving it alone when it wants to be. The mouse should take care not to cause pain to this wonderful friend, whether by sarcasm or infidelity, because it is a very lucky mouse indeed to have found such a compliant, affectionate partner.

THE YEAR
OF THE
OX

CHOU

OX YEARS

1901	February 19 to February 7, 1902
1913	February 6 to January 25, 1914
1925	January 24 to February 12, 1926
1937	February 11 to January 30, 1938
1949	January 29 to February 16, 1950
1961	February 15 to February 4, 1962
1973	February 3 to January 22, 1974
1985	February 20 to February 8, 1986
1997	February 7 to January 27, 1998
2009	January 26 to February 13, 2010
2021	February 12 to January 31, 2022
2033	January 31 to February 18, 2034
2045	February 17 to February 5, 2046

ASSOCIATIONS

EARTHLY BRANCH CHARACTER: *Chou* denotes a connection or joint, and is thus associated with sequence, series, and combination, and by extension with strength and stability. The essence of those born in the Year of the Ox is strength of the deep, dark, yin variety, which is characterized by endurance. They are faithful and powerful, but can be inflexible, unable to back down a road once they have advanced on it, never thinking of stepping aside.

ANIMAL: Chinese Buddhists say that cattle, with their kind and uncomplaining strength, were sent to humanity by the Goddess of Mercy, Guan Yin, and most Buddhists refrain from eating beef as a sign of love and respect for this noble and gentle animal. The ox is also a symbol of parental love in China, because of the tenderness with which it licks its calf.

The ox *(niu)* is stubborn and strong-minded, enduring and hard-working. It is also much more intelligent than it looks, although its intelligence is not of the kind that always sees two sides to every question. Ox people are good at planning, excellent in defensive tactics, and alert and careful in waiting out a situation as they weigh the risks, avoiding premature action. Once they make up their minds to do something they are strong and instinctive, and proceed step by step, without fear, enduring whatever obstacles may lie ahead. Patience and hard work are their keys to unlocking difficulties. They are deeply attached to home and family, especially their children.

ORDER: The second position in the Chinese zodiac is the strongest, and ox people are capable of breaking through to the most important leadership positions in any field as long as they can skillfully maintain peace and harmony among the elements of growth. To do this they must learn to recognize the value of contradictory ideas, and give their subordinates room to try out new things and stretch their imaginations. Otherwise they may find themselves and their organizations stuck in the mud, neither advancing nor retreating.

ELEMENT: Earth, in harmony with Metal, in conflict with Water, overcoming Fire and subjected to Wood. This element governs the ox person's deep attachment to home and family, a prime motivation in the activities and emotions of those born in this year. Oxen are also deeply bonded to earth itself: they are at their best in activities related to land, fertility, plants, and minerals. Home and earth are the great sources of the ox's strength; its weaknesses come from its inflexibility, which can harm both the ox and those who depend on it.

STAR GROUP: The Palace of the Year of the Ox is ruled by the Earth Star (Saturn), and houses three Lodges or Star-Spirits: Mei, Gei, and Dao, corresponding to stars in the Western constellations of Scorpio and Sagittarius. There is potential for major conflict, based on these star associations, with those born in the Year of the Ram, whose bright yang energy can be every bit as unbending as the ox's yin. Generally, conflict will come from those who are like the ox in this respect; ox people learn that their supporters tend to be more complex characters who admire their courage and consistency without sharing it.

FAVORABLE DIRECTION: North-northeast; ox people will obtain the most successful results with projects and journeys oriented a third of the way east from due north. If they are building or remodeling a home, a favorite activity of the highly domesticated oxen, they may like to have it backing northward, angled partly toward the east; this will help their own particular *qi* of prosperity to flow inside and remain. Traveling in China, they will enjoy escaping the summer heat as the emperors did by making the pretty journey to Chengde, and they may decide to keep going, being stubborn oxen, until they reach the cooler landscapes of Manchuria.

FAVORABLE MONTH: Late February to early March, the time after the long hibernation of quietness and tranquility, when all the insects, animals, and plants are slowly resurrecting. During this period ox people are charged with renewed energy, new ideas, exciting projects, and perhaps intimate desires. It is the time to think seriously and take advantage of earlier planning; the time for action is just around the corner.

FAVORABLE HOUR: 1:00 AM to 3:00 AM, the peaceful early hours of the day, consecrated to rest and the conservation of energy for action when the dawn arrives. This is the time when the yin force is still dominant but beginning to decline; the ox people, whose energy is primarily yin, are at peace as their great strength accumulates to push them past whatever obstacles arise in the day.

FAVORABLE NUMBERS: 1, 3, 5, 12, 15, 33, 35, 51, 53.

THE WHOLE PERSON

CHARACTER: Under a facade of equal parts stability, charm, calm, and awkwardness, ox people often surprise others with their rigorous intelligence. Ox people are open and positive by nature, and extend warmth and friendship to all around them. They are highly sensitive to the environment and climatic change and love the outdoors; they are often in the forefront of those who are concerned about the environmental issues upon which our survival and prosperity in future generations depend.

Their stubbornness, the only facet of their personalities that is perceived by others as negative, is truly awesome: having chosen a goal, they can almost never be deflected from it.

EMOTIONS: Ox people are even-tempered and home-oriented, in need of a stable environment at home and at work. They are intense, and their strong positive regard for home and family can show up as extreme possessiveness. They are friendly, peaceable, and good team players. Despite their quiet nature, they love parties and social activities. With all the hard work they do, they deserve relaxing entertainment and leisure that does not interfere with their privacy and peace of mind.

Conservative and cautious, they hate moving from one place to another; they are homebodies who prefer to stay in one place for a long time, beautifying their home with equal attention to comfort and pride.

WEAKNESSES: Never underestimate the charge of a raging bull and its goring horns. Ox people can be quietly manipulative, but the real danger is when their orientation to home leads to possessiveness, obsession, and authoritarianism, and this must be guarded against. At worst, and this is very rare, the ox person can combine extremes of fanaticism, blind anger, and possessiveness to a degree that is virtually inhuman—Napoleon and Hitler were both oxen. The strategy for rising above such dangers is to overcome hurt feelings and hurtful events with healthy views, and to take the high ground against obstacles.

LIFESTYLE: It is rare to find an ox person willing to be the first to try out trendy clothes and new gadgets. They generally wait and see, saying that if things are doing the job, why replace them? They are fond of sweets and snacks, and need to guard against overeating. What they enjoy most of all is being outdoors, hiking, camping, and taking in the view.

FAMOUS OX PEOPLE: Hans Christian Andersen, Johann Sebastian Bach, Charles Chaplin, Jean Cocteau, Sammy Davis, Jr., Marlene Dietrich, Walt Disney, Clark Gable, George Gershwin, Helen Hayes, Jascha Heifetz, Hermann Hesse, Adolf Hitler, Emperor Kangxi, Margaret Mead, Napoleon, Paul Newman, Robert Redford, Auguste Renoir, Artur Rubinstein, Peter Paul Rubens, Vincent van Gogh, Daniel Webster, William Butler Yeats.

OX PEOPLE BORN IN...

Note: Western-calendar months are given as approximations only; to find a birth moon according to the Chinese lunisolar calendar, consult the chart on pp. 30–45.

FIRST MOON (FEBRUARY): Still somewhat under the influence of the previous Year of the Mouse, they are less stubborn and self-confident than most ox people. They are artistic, creative, individualistic and freethinking, and very strong and expressive in their likes and dislikes. They tend to be quiet but restless, sensitive, and eccentric, and sometimes very conscious of personal cleanliness and cosmetics. They enjoy beautiful things, well designed and attractively presented, and acquire them very selectively.

SECOND MOON (MARCH): Contradictory in thought and character, sensitive and awkward at the same time, they are nevertheless skillful people who often turn their contradictory views into creative artistic and intellectual work. They are good at music, literature, dance, design, collecting antiques, and playing card games. Because of the ox-like stubbornness they invest in their creative work and their controversial ideas, they invite betrayal and deception.

THIRD MOON (APRIL): Very independent people and often loners, their confidence makes them easily lose perspective and ignore good advice from friends who care for them. Frustration and trouble can be their lot, especially in youth. Ox persons born in this month are disturbed by its young yang energy, which can distract them from their goals and affect them internally. They need to pay close attention to diet and health, preserving themselves for better times in mid-life and later.

FOURTH MOON (MAY): These oxen are led by the old yin force of this month to take a more objective view of life. They are drawn to concentration and competition, and are often intellectuals, independent in thought and manner. Many of them are successful in their fields; organized and cautious, they make good researchers and scholars. They are also charming, beautiful, and spoiled, and may be somewhat impractical.

FIFTH MOON (JUNE): These are people who tend to be attracted by extremes instead of looking for the center. Radical and unpredictable, their mixture of hot and cold can cause frustration and misunderstanding among friends. They are likely to suffer a rocky and unsettling mid-life crisis, but will overcome it. They are not easy to live with, being often eccentric and unreasonable, but they are the most interesting and witty ox people, full of surprises.

SIXTH MOON (JULY): Youthful oxen, more likely to be sexually promiscuous than others, they are very steady and intelligent in career matters, and are likely to have early successes in life. Although they appear somewhat careless in personal matters, they long for an emotional stability to match their general prosperity, and will not be happy until they finally settle down.

SEVENTH MOON (AUGUST): Highly artistic and independent, these ox people seem calm and gentle on the outside, but in reality they are restless and contradictory, suffering from silent rages. They mix strong creativity and imagination with good common sense. Once they have decided to work on something they will keep trying regardless of obstacles, pursuing their ends with energy and strength; these oxen are not often quitters.

EIGHTH MOON (SEPTEMBER): Active, talkative, friendly and entertaining, they enjoy being at the center of attention. But they are loners, refusing to be tied down by anyone or anything, and need to be tamed. They are as home-oriented as other oxen, however, devoting much energy to the creation of a beautiful retreat in their house or apartment. The problem is that they may be too fussy to find someone to share it with.

NINTH MOON (OCTOBER): Sensitive and passionate, soft-hearted and friendly, they are subject to being taken advantage of by friends unless they can learn to say no, and this may cause them trouble in life. Fortunately, they can overcome this, and their resourcefulness, skill, and intelligence, allows them to emerge as winning competitors.

TENTH MOON (NOVEMBER): These are confident, honest people. Consistent, but also   idealistic perfectionists, they concentrate hard on whatever they do and are likely to succeed. Many of them are self-employed or occupy leadership positions. They are the type to fall in love at first sight, and can be very possessive and controlling, but they are also honest and faithful to friends and family.

ELEVENTH MOON (DECEMBER): Quiet, contemplative, and very aggressive at the same time, they are talented leaders, friendly but reserved, who love to accumulate power and wealth through deep thinking and planning. Their challenge and temptation is addiction in all its forms—food, alcohol, smoking, drugs, cars, money, sex, and power.

TWELFTH MOON (JANUARY OF FOLLOWING YEAR): These oxen are good, reliable, productive people, but also competitive and self-centered. They are hard-working and quiet but dislike criticism of any kind, even positive. Especially when young, they are inclined to think they can change the whole world with their own two hands. However, they will learn from early blunders, and become more mellow and flexible in attitude and practice, and thus more successful, in later life.

THE LIFE CYCLE

HEALTH: Ox people are generally very healthy, but must guard against abusing their bodies by neglect and carelessness, especially when young. Because they know themselves to be reliable, honest, and stable, they think they can safely experiment with drugs, alcohol, and fast driving, but their obsessive character makes them liable to addiction. Ox people need to pay attention to stomach and respiratory problems, as well as complications and problems related to excessive drinking, smoking, and unhealthy diet. They are especially vulnerable to intestinal problems and extremes of hot or cold weather.

MONEY: Analytical and quietly aggressive, possessed of strength, energy, and skill at patient observation and long-term planning, ox people know how to play the money game well. They are adept at finance, management, real estate, and development. They are conservative and defensive players in money and investment ventures. Their association with the

Earth element and love of nature suggests that activity in land, fertility, plants, and minerals is favorable for investment. They are not big spenders, and conscious of saving for a rainy day or for retirement.

CAREER: With their intelligence, patience, stability, and diligence, ox people are suited to any career they choose, but may be particularly creative and skillful with their hands, excelling at trades ranging from arts and crafts, carpentry and drafting, to work as mechanics, sculptors and dentists. You will find oxen successful as architects, artists, educators, engineers, jewelers; they are also active in financial services, management, farming, geology, health care, real estate, the military, politics, technology, and public relations.

LOVE: In love, ox people can be intense and possessive. Their slow, patient, consistent character attracts the opposite type, those who are variable and less secure. Taking the cue from their orientation to nature, they learn to plow the land and keep the trees of love growing prosperously into fruitful orchards.

In love quarrels and fights, oxen are solid defenders with plenty of strength and intelligence to guard their territory. But they must beware of blind obsessions and possessiveness carried to extremes. It is better for them to leave their options open and let more air and flexibility into their orchards so that other trees and flowers may bloom—let the life force, *qi*, flow according to its own course and, like water, find its own level.

OX PARTNERS BORN IN
THE YEAR OF THE...

MOUSE: The mercurial mouse person provides plenty of entertainment for the ox, but is at heart practical enough that the ox will not get too nervous; they are very different, but in ways that complement each other, and at a deeper level they are actually rather similar. There is potential here for a very stable relationship.

OX: It is hard for two oxen to become romantically involved with each other—who is going to make the first move? When they do, however, it is likely to be a wonderfully, though quietly happy relationship. Only those oxen who have the same ideas about everything already will get together in the first place, so their stubbornness will not bring them into quarrels with each other, only with everyone else.

TIGER: Both tiger and ox are simultaneously aggressive and defensive, as well as overly fond of power. With aims in life that tend to be totally different, they find each other hard to understand, and the inevitable quarrels lead nowhere. It will be very difficult for the ox to get anything positive from this relationship, and this is made worse by the fact that the tiger does get something it wants—a stable, happy home—which it then takes for granted and proceeds to ignore.

RABBIT: The rabbit's attraction to the ox may be only superficial, and because it expects pampering and indulgence where the ox wants to give stability and a clear set of rules, there will be misunderstandings. But if the rabbit is patient and tolerant, difficulties can be overcome. When this relationship works at all it works very well, for the long term, with warmth and caring.

DRAGON: This relationship may look more like a battle than a romance; indeed, it is a heavyweight championship between the brute ox strength and the dragon's fancy feints and footwork. The ox hates to give up, however, and in the end it may be a good match, and should not be prejudged.

SNAKE: Ox and snake communicate well, the mature yin of the one balancing the rising yang of the other. This can be a very harmonious, long-lasting relationship. The ox will have to learn to moderate its jealous rages, and unfortunately they are sometimes justified. It may be very difficult for both parties to wait out the early storms, but there is calm, prosperous sailing ahead for those who do.

HORSE: It is impossible for the ox to tame the swift and clever horse; both are good kickers, but the horse is faster. In a business relationship or casual friendship, they get along, often very well, but they cannot be connected romantically without severe suffering for the ox. The fact is that the horse just doesn't care that much about love after the conquest is made, and the ox has little to offer that it really wants.

RAM: The astrological conflict between these two animals means that a relationship will be rough going from beginning to end. Even the exceptionally patient ox should be very cautious in making an exclusive commitment without keeping other irons in the love-fire, and should also beware of tearing down the whole stable in pursuit of a single goal!

MONKEY: Ox and monkey will work well together. The monkey's innocent pleasure in the most outrageous sexual hijinks breaks down ox's inhibitions and teaches it things it never suspected about having a good time. It takes time for the monkey to settle into a relationship, however, and the ox is advised to be patient and let things happen.

ROOSTER: These two are definitely good for each other: one crows to set everyone to work, and the other draws the plow. Not everyone can get along with the nagging rooster, but the irritation it provides is of a kind that the ox is quite well-equipped to handle. Having someone understand it so well, without being at all wimpy, may soften the rooster a bit.

DOG: Nobody ties the dog down except the dog itself, in a freely chosen relationship. The conflicting yin energies of ox and dog are doomed to conflict, with a big communication problem. The ox has to make a lot of compromises to make this romance work—perhaps too many for it to be worthwhile.

PIG: Not everybody gets along with the kindly, friendly pig; the ox, in particular, does not quite see the point. If they happen to get together, though, they can have a good time. Don't expect miracles from this relationship; ox and pig will need plenty of adjustments to make it work. But if there are enough sparks of excitement to get the fire burning, they can certainly cook a good meal together, and the ox loves good home cooking.

THE YEAR
OF THE
TIGER

YIN

TIGER YEARS

1902	February 8 to January 28, 1903
1914	January 26 to February 13, 1915
1926	February 13 to February 1, 1927
1938	January 31 to February 18, 1939
1950	February 17 to February 5, 1951
1962	February 5 to January 24, 1963
1974	January 23 to February 10, 1975
1986	February 9 to January 28, 1987
1998	January 28 to February 15, 1999
2010	February 14 to February 2, 2011
2022	February 1 to January 21, 2023
2034	February 19 to February 7, 2035
2046	February 6 to January 25, 2047

ASSOCIATIONS

EARTHLY BRANCH CHARACTER: *Yin* represents a man standing somewhat stiffly, wearing a cap, with his hands upraised in salutation. It denotes ritual politeness, the paying of honor, and therefore the inspiration of respect and reverence; by extension, it suggests both positions and attitudes of leadership. The word is pronounced in Chinese with a rising tone, not to be confused with the yin, pronounced with a high level tone, that refers to the dark female power.

The essence of people born in this year is nobility: they are always on the quest for something bigger and more beautiful than their own personal advantage, and their values, like those of the heroes of classical epics, may seem extravagant to more humble people. This does not mean that they are in any sense pompous or boring—they are witty companions, full of fun and excitement—but that they are always inclined to feel themselves above petty concerns.

ANIMAL: In Chinese tradition, the noble tiger (*hu*) is the king of all animals, and so ferocious that it can be combatted only by someone who is in such a state of despair that he no longer cares whether he lives or dies, like the hero Wu Song in the novel *Water Margin*. More objectively, it is known to be an alert, curious beast, always ready to take bold action when the opportunity presents itself and the timing is right. It is a mighty hunter, roaming the night, and some say that tiger people born in the night hours are fiercer than those born in the daytime.

People born in the Year of the Tiger are calm and cool until the moment for action arrives, maintaining a hidden agenda of plots for advancement, and quick and unpredictable when they move. They are highly intelligent and optimistic, and fearlessly explore, bargain, and conquer in any type of business, investment, or creative work.

ORDER: The Year of the Tiger is in the third position of the Chinese zodiac, one of high honor and power. Simultaneously creative and destructive, taking stances that are both offensive and defensive, their strength and alertness often make people born in this year excellent achievers, even running several different careers or multiple businesses at the same time. On the other hand, their restlessness makes them troublemakers and not always trustworthy. Their leadership abilities, however, are beyond question, and many will rise very high.

ELEMENT: Wood, in complementary relation to Water, supportive of Fire, but in conflict with Metal and Earth. Tigers are strong, consistent, and victorious by nature, with the strength of trees, which neither bend nor break. They draw extra reserves of strength from their lairs and families to bring with them on the hunt. Their weaknesses stem from their sense of superiority to others, which leads them to see their enemies as relatively simple-minded, and also from their curiosity—since they are after all only very large and powerful cats—which entices them to leave safe places and lures them into traps.

STAR GROUP: The Palace of the Year of the Tiger is ruled by the Wood Star (Jupiter), and houses four important Lodges or Star-Spirits: Ti, Fang, Xin and Yi, corresponding to stars in Libra, Antares and Scorpio. Astrologically, there is a potential for major conflict between tigers and those born in the Year of the Monkey, and the tiger is likely to be the loser in such conflicts, because the monkey's element, Metal, threatens the tiger's Wood. This needs to be guarded against with caution and respect for monkey people. In general, their conflicts are with those less idealistic than themselves, whose motives they do not clearly understand. They draw support from their many admirers, and people in sympathy with their ideals.

FAVORABLE DIRECTION: East-Northeast. Plans that are oriented toward the sector one-third northward from due East will have successful results. Traveling in China, tiger people will not want to miss Shandong, where they can pay their respects to the noble Confucius at his birthplace in Qufu, and relax—why not, for once?—on the beaches of Qingdao, with a glass of the splendid beer from the local brewery founded by Germans toward the end of the last century.

FAVORABLE MONTH: Mid-March to mid-April, in the beautiful springtime, when animals are coming out of their long hibernation, buds are bursting into leaves, and everything is stirring toward new activities. Tigers are happy to extend their territorial reach and sphere of influence in anticipation of good hunting and colorful events in the coming months.

FAVORABLE HOUR: 3:00 AM to 5:00 AM, a quiet time for sleep and the conservation of energy and strength, preparing for action at the coming of the dawn. This is the time when the bright yang force grows in concealment, as the sun prepares to rise. The active tigers are the yang power of the night, but tiger people should use this time to gain the necessary peace and balance to enhance inner harmony, endurance, and self-protection. It is a time to contemplate, reflect and plan for the next step toward the achievement of long-term goals, to make the most productive use of the tiger's excess of energy.

FAVORABLE NUMBERS: 4, 5, 9, 13, 34, 44, 45, 54.

THE WHOLE PERSON

CHARACTER: Tiger people embrace life with vigor and creativity, and have a certain magnetism and attractiveness that few can resist and no one can ignore. Proud and confident, they are smooth talkers and skilled gossips, but this light-heartedness is belied by their strength as well as their capacity for quickly acquiring new information and ideas.

Their ability and calm observation win praise wherever they go, and stir up envy among friends and enemies alike. They are egotistical, dominating, cool, calculating, aloof, and showy, and know how to make good use of these qualities, positioning themselves as leaders and revolutionaries in life and work. Beware of their big smiles and ceaseless energy, seeking advances and leaving no stone unturned. They love to be the commanding generals on the battlefield, charging forward to victory or defeat.

EMOTIONS: Tigers are emotionally restless, seeking relentlessly to climb the mountaintops, peak after peak. Even at the height of their power they may fall into unhappiness and discontent, feeling lonely, isolated, empty and miserable. Protective and territorial, they will walk ten miles out and ten miles back to defend their ground, fearlessly, against intruders and competitors, but they are not usually very good at staying home. They are demanding and opportunistic, and sometimes even unfaithful, always keeping their eyes on a better deal or another new chance. They are incapable of dealing with solitude and loneliness.

WEAKNESSES: The tiger's tendency to move forward stealthily and secretively on a hidden agenda can be dangerous, leading it into baited traps and forbidden ground in which even a tiger might get stuck. More dangerous for others is their excess of power, which some tigers may be inclined to abuse. Fortunately, even a tiger can be tamed—don't forget that it is a member of the cat family, though a dangerous one. Under the right circumstances these big cats can be so well behaved that their wild killer nature becomes invisible; we love as well as fear them.

LIFESTYLE: Tiger people love good parties, food, clothes, dazzling entertainments, and fun with friends, both for their own enjoyment and the opportunity to make waves and gain attention. They are especially fond of beautiful things and environments, and are convinced that money is there to be spent—they can always make more tomorrow. Witty and humorous, they are always willing to try out new trends with curiosity and enthusiasm.

FAMOUS TIGER PEOPLE: Ludwig van Beethoven, Elizabeth Barrett Browning, Marie Curie, Isadora Duncan, Dwight D. Eisenhower, Francesco Goya, Charles de Gaulle, Allen Ginsberg, Ho Chi Minh, Charles Lindbergh, Louis XIV, Marilyn Monroe, Karl Marx, Vaslav Nijinsky, Niccolò Paganini, Man Ray, Sun Yat-sen, Dylan Thomas, Oscar Wilde, William Wordsworth.

TIGER PEOPLE BORN IN THE...

Note: Western-calendar months are given as approximations only; to find a birth moon according to the Chinese lunisolar calendar, consult the chart on pp. 30–45.

FIRST MOON (FEBRUARY): These tigers are born when the previous Year of the Ox is still exercising its patient influence. They are reserved, quiet and stubborn. Friendly, and with less of a tendency to be showoffs than other tigers, they are slow in communication but observant and perceptive, very strong and passionate, and adventurous in their youth. Home-oriented, and good home-makers when the time comes, it is wise for them to wait until after mid-life to settle down.

SECOND MOON (MARCH): Quick and alert in action, they do not like to dilute their ideas with too much thinking and worrying, but go right out to face the challenges at hand with a bluntness that is unlike the sharp approach of most tigers. Very capable, courageous, swift, intelligent and unyielding, they inspire great love in friends and great hatred in enemies.

THIRD MOON (APRIL): Passionate and sensitive, daring, generous, and caring, they may neglect themselves in their commitment to helping others, and this may cost them some degree of success and respect, especially in early life. Their restlessness and fearlessness frightens those close to them. In all the excitement, they may lose their objectivity, and this will cause trouble and frustration, but these young tigers will push on to win.

FOURTH MOON (MAY): These tigers are optimistic, individualistic, and hard-working. They enjoy social gatherings and activities, and their friends and fellow hobbyists keep them busy all day long. Childlike in their attitudes to life, they are passionate lovers but not always faithful to a single partner.

FIFTH MOON (JUNE): Open, optimistic, good-hearted, they love parties and are loved by friends. They can be quite subjective and opinionated about things, but are also sometimes blocked briefly by indecision; this is soon overcome as they push for another horizon. Generally quiet, calm, and strong-minded, they are loners who leave home early to establish their own lairs and territories. Winning admiration wherever they go, capable of managing two careers at a time and doing well in both, they are good people, though difficult to live with.

SIXTH MOON (JULY): Generally these are lucky tigers, with comfortable childhoods and perhaps a modest inheritance. They are strong and open-minded, but with their innate restlessness and lack of a contemplative nature, they can be careless and awkward in social relations. Their early chasing after success is marked by ups and downs and twists and turns, but they remain fearless, and after mid-life they will be very capable and attain what they are looking for.

SEVENTH MOON (AUGUST): Good planners and quick players, these tigers are lucky and successful in life, especially as they get older. The mid-life period could be the decisive one in getting on the right track for the attainment of their goals. They can work ceaselessly and fearlessly to benefit humanity, and their born leadership can easily turn into a great creative force.

EIGHTH MOON (SEPTEMBER): Perceptive and instinctive, tigers born in this moon are so independent that they hate to receive even the help that is rightfully theirs. They tend to be very artistic and responsive to dance and music. They have a great reservoir of creative yin energy waiting to be used and expressed, and their romances tend to be very uneven and jumpy, as they think more about their artistic lives than their love lives.

NINTH MOON (OCTOBER): Quiet when working, yet highly excitable in social activities, they pursue their ideals with intensity and passion. Physical beauty and presentation are very important to them; they are beautiful themselves, childlike in certain ways, and very playful at times. Friends may perceive them as insensitive and immature.

TENTH MOON (NOVEMBER): Lucky tigers, who do things well and achieve success in life, they are frank, bold and daring. They dislike being occupied with details and leave them to their partners, but keep marching on with aggression and strength, always looking for new frontiers, possibilities, and freedom. They are difficult to tie down, and fond of arguing with friends, pushing their points of view without awareness of the trouble they may be causing.

ELEVENTH MOON (DECEMBER): Stubborn and aggressive, they are runaround types, always looking out for a good catch. They like to see and to conquer and do not care to take advice, even if they can see that it is sound. These are the most active and dangerous tigers; they must be careful with alcohol, driving, and combining the two: slow down and stay sober!

TWELFTH MOON (JANUARY OF FOLLOWING YEAR): Confident tigers, full of quiet aggression aimed constantly at the highest conquerable ground, they are calm in appearance and very clever. Good at persuading others, like a friendly tiger with a good catch in view, they are very successful career people, though their overconfidence and energy also bring them lots of enemies. They may lead unhappy lives if their competitiveness and hunger for glory does not allow them to enjoy contentment.

THE LIFE CYCLE

HEALTH: Most tigers are physically in tune and athletically gifted. Outdoor exercise and a good environment are their secrets for maintaining fitness and health, providing them with the strength and energy to pursue their careers with success. Their love of novelty indicates that they should watch out for excess in eating, drinking, drugs, gambling, fast driving, and so on. Generally speaking, they do not have many serious illnesses, but suffer more from self-inflicted ailments that arise out of the worries and internal conflicts that they are always busy thinking about.

MONEY: Cautious about guarding what they have, alert and protective, many tigers are aggressive and brave in terms of money, and they will prosper if the timing and temperature are right and the ingredients are good. They are good fighters and know all the pitfalls of the war games of the financial world. They can divert their restless minds into looking out for new signs and trends, but must care for their own nests; long-term strategies and goals are required for young cubs to prosper. They are at their best if they can achieve balance and perspective and moderate the greed of conquest.

CAREER: With their talent, efficiency, aggressiveness, and leadership ability, tigers fit into all sorts of careers; you will find them succeeding especially as artists, businesspeople, critics, dancers, financiers, engineers, journalists, musicians, poets, public relations workers, politicians, travel agents, and in the military, science, medicine, and technology.

LOVE: Romantically intense and possessive, tiger people enjoy sex and love. They may not be loyal or faithful, as their restless and emotional character constantly draws them to new attractions, and anything warm, beautiful, sexy, or desirable will not escape their notice. Moreover, because of their hatred of solitude and the feeling of being at their best when on the hunt, they are always chasing after someone.

TIGER PARTNERS BORN IN
THE YEAR OF THE...

MOUSE: The mouse is very difficult for the tiger to catch, too swift and small, and too cynical, perhaps, to be seduced by admiration for the tiger's splendid qualities. Once caught, however, it may well reform; the tiger can be forgiven if it gives up hope, but it need not do so.

OX: The tiger may be attracted by the stability the ox provides at the beginning, but it will get bored, and, worse, may start feeling caged. If this relationship does not come to an early end, it is likely to get unpleasant and even bitter, and very difficult to break off cleanly.

TIGER: Two tigers will not get along smoothly; they need much compromise and forgiveness to avoid biting each other's tails. At the same time, there is a lot of mutual understanding to work with, each partner having sympathy with the other's ideals, and they can end up happy together.

RABBIT: It is not the rabbit's idea of happiness to sit around the house while its mate ranges the wild world looking for prey, and it will be restless in this relationship. The tiger will have to be very patient, attentive, and thoughtful while the rabbit makes up its mind, which can take a very long time in this case. In the end, there is considerable potential for happiness, because each supplies something the other lacks.

DRAGON: There will be clashes, and sometimes very dramatic ones, because both animals are equally powerful. Once tiger gives up on the idea of taming the dragon and accepts the possibility of being the less showy partner—which is not easy for tigers to do, used as they are to unquestioned dominance— there is much mutual sympathy to build on, and they make a good-looking couple.

SNAKE: The tiger is strongly attracted to this sexy partner, but the snake is probably not especially interested, and this makes things complicated. This relationship is considered a poor gamble on both sides, although it is very hard for the tiger to give up.

HORSE: The horse-tiger relationship may seem a little too easy, as neither side asks too much from the other and they have much in common. Then again, there is the question of who is going to stay home while these two heroes wander the world looking for injustice. Tiger will have to learn to accept a certain amount of instability and sometimes a high level of conflict.

RAM: The ram may be attracted to the tiger's noble quest in life, but also suspicious as to whether it is genuine. The tiger, meanwhile, will need to pay attention to the ram's complex set of behavioral rules, and can find the whole thing more frustrating than it is worth. Working it out will be difficult.

MONKEY: The tiger who has the unusual idea of being attracted to a monkey will be very frustrated as the monkey swings from tree to tree, continually evading the tiger's grasp. This is to be considered a good outcome; if they get together at last, the star-crossed difficulties can be devastating.

ROOSTER: If the rooster is chasing the tiger, the outcome is not likely to be good for either, because these two have great difficulty communicating. Ultimately this is unlikely to be a case of genuine attraction, and more probably a game for both sides.

DOG: This relationship should lead to marriage. The dog fearlessly guards the household while tiger prowls the neighborhood, looking for ways of bringing prosperity to the family. They respect one another and have a great deal of mutual understanding. There will undoubtedly be quarrels, but nothing to change the basic situation.

PIG : The danger in a relationship with pig is that the tiger will be too fierce and the pig too nervous, afraid of being eaten. It is unwise for the tiger to move too fast: if it remains gentle and understanding it can build a very happy life with this unassuming and appreciative partner. The pig's sense of fun also helps the tiger to lighten up.

THE YEAR OF THE RABBIT

MAO

RABBIT YEARS

1903	January 29 to February 15, 1904
1915	February 14 to February 2, 1916
1927	February 2 to January 22, 1928
1939	February 19 to February 7, 1940
1951	February 6 to January 26, 1952
1963	January 25 to February 12, 1964
1975	February 11 to January 30, 1976
1987	January 29 to February 16, 1988
1999	February 16 to February 4, 2000
2011	February 3 to January 22, 2012
2023	January 22 to February 9, 2024
2035	February 8 to January 27, 2036
2047	January 26 to February 13, 2048

ASSOCIATIONS

EARTHLY BRANCH CHARACTER: *Mao* is an obscure character in origin, having become confused in the course of the evolution of written Chinese with a number of other characters. It signifies a mortise, that is the trapezoidal groove that makes the female side of a dovetail joint, which holds fast to the other side (the tenon) without being glued or nailed to it, and is easily removed when the time comes to take the assembly apart. The essence of those born in this year is detachment; they thrive in the middle of all kinds of social goings-on but rarely seem to be fully engaged in them. Warm, friendly and alert, they tend nevertheless to avoid close emotional involvement, and prefer to maintain their lives at a calm, even pace, keeping quiet, even-tempered, and low-keyed.

ANIMAL: The rabbit *(tu)* is known to be most clever and intelligent, swift in thought and in action. Chinese folk wisdom maintains that it always has three exits to its burrow, enabling it to escape any tragedy. Those born in the Year of the Rabbit are wild by nature, wily and quick, making them difficult to domesticate. They are also on the timorous side, and in confrontations more likely to run than stand and fight. This does not mean that it is easy to take advantage of them; leading their enemies on a chase through bogs and brambles is their way of fighting, and it can be very effective.

A more naive story holds that rabbits conceive their young without intercourse, through the sensitive touch of the doe licking the buck's hair; you don't have to know much about rabbits to know that this is far from true. Sexy as they are, however, rabbit people do have a tendency to sentimentality, the unearned emotion; this is one of the things that makes them marvellous storytellers, alongside their sophistication in matters of the arts. They are wonderful, entertaining, and gentle friends, and superb organizers when things are going well, but they may not respond as well in a crisis that requires them to suffer along with others.

ORDER: The fourth position in the Chinese zodiac is a gentle but strong and radiant position. The warmth of rabbit people combines with endurance and sensitivity, cleverness and flexibility, to provide inner strength and unity. As leaders, their special and unique skill is to establish a common purpose and draw others into the maintenance of harmony and prosperity.

ELEMENT: Wood, which complements Water, the essence of life and action, and gives birth to Fire, which provides the energy for action. Water, which also connotes money and prosperity, nourishes Wood. Metal, which has associations with weapons, aggression, greed, and extremism, is in conflict with Wood, oppressing it by its weight. Rabbit people are advised to take safe and conservative strategies and to avoid heavy, risk-taking approaches; their strength comes from whatever grows gently and gradually, and they must shore it up in order to cope with their weaknesses, which arise in moments of crisis.

STAR GROUP: The Fire Star (Mars) rules the Palace of the Year of the Rabbit, which houses three Lodges or Star-Spirits: Jiao, Kang, and Ti, corresponding to stars within Spica, Virgo, and Libra. These stars warn that rabbit people are potentially in major conflict with those born in the Year of the Rooster. At a more general level, rabbit people tend to avoid conflict altogether, but it comes to them inevitably from the bullies of the world, who see them as easy victims. Luckily the bullies are often mistaken, as anyone who has ever tried to chase a rabbit knows. Many friends find their kind and charming nature irresistible, and as long as they make an effort to hold on to those friends, they will be assured of wide support in time of need.

FAVORABLE DIRECTION: East, home of the Green Dragon in Chinese mythology, whose element is Water and which governs the spring: a symbol for youth, energy, strength, honor, and good luck. Projects oriented to the east will turn out well for rabbit people, with the Green Dragon as an ally of good omen for their ideas, plans, and careers. Traveling in China, they should not miss the chance to cruise on the ancient Grand Canal to the beautiful lakes and gardens of Yangzhou.

FAVORABLE MONTH: Mid-April to Mid-May, when plants are exploding into flower and filling the fields with intoxicating scents, and animals are alternately dreamy and aggressive with sexual excitement. The rabbit, young or old, is at its peak in this period, ready to release the energy it has been patiently accumulating; it is time for the fulfillment of desire. In the dreamy springtime, rabbit people may give in to the temptation of indulging their fantasies, but they will pay a heavy price if this is not tied to creative action.

FAVORABLE HOUR: 5:00 A M to 7:00 A M, when you can see the sun rising from the Green Dragon's lair in the east, but the yin power at its most mature and wise phase, dominates—the most magical, glorious, and important time of the day. Rabbits leave their nests early, making the most of the time when the fiercer yang creatures are still rubbing the sleep from their eyes; rabbit people should be especially alert, tapping the secret wisdom and resources that only they possess at this time of day. This is also the hour of reveille, whence the modern meaning of the character *mao* as the verb of mustering and summoning; those born in this year are often called on to summon others into service, in spite of their meekness, or because of their cool rationality.

FAVORABLE NUMBERS: 1, 3, 5, 9, 15, 19, 35.

THE WHOLE PERSON

CHARACTER: Warm, friendly, intelligent, and confident, rabbit people win admiration and acceptance wherever they go. They tend to have remarkable insight into creative and detail work, and to be gifted and diplomatic in dealing with people. With their alertness, analytic ability, and sensitivity, they may quietly and skillfully manipulate a situation for their own gain, but most are trustworthy, friendly, goodhearted, and attentive, genuinely concerned with the needs of others.

Natural comedians with positive energy, rabbits make naughty and hilarious conversationalists and storytellers, shine at parties and other social activities, and are great traveling companions. They work hard and productively, and are often creative hobbyists, skillful with their hands, and first-class cooks.

EMOTIONS: The rabbit is by nature even-tempered, calm, and emotionally low-keyed, with a remarkable ability to heal from psychological wounds as well as physical ones. Rabbit people often seem detached, observers rather than participants, and they often exploit this quality as social-anthropological poets, field experts, and writers on human affairs. However, they dislike solitude and prefer to spend time with friends and lovers.

WEAKNESSES: Most rabbit people dislike unwanted disturbances and complicated details, preferring the smooth and gently graded paths to growth in life and work. These easy roads are full of traps to catch them in conflict, indecision, and confusion, and can be detours into illusion and disappointment. Materialism in general, and giving too much of a priority to comfort and beauty, are a source of temptation, especially when reactive rabbits fail to plan for the long term and plunge into the high life and high-risk speculation. They must avoid conflict with the way of Metal and look for nourishment from Water.

LIFESTYLE: Rabbit people are tremendously fond of taking care of their outsides with fragrances and skin care products, jewelry, clothing, and luxurious accessories, and put a high priority on their physical presentation. There is really no kind of shopping they dislike, whether it is for clothes and cosmetics, fitness equipment or cooking gadgets, cars, exotic plants, or audiovisual systems and computers.

Sensitive and friendly to the environment, they enjoy camping, backpacking, and journeying in the wilderness. Foreign travel also pleases them, and they pick up the most entertaining stories about local customs and sights, later to be used at a party to charm an unsuspecting guest. At home, they hang out in museums, galleries, dance studios, and music halls, carrying on their artistic and cultural education.

FAMOUS RABBIT PEOPLE: Marie Antoinette, Agatha Christie, Albert Einstein, Henry Wadsworth Longfellow, Paul Klee, Arthur Miller,

Emperor Qianlong, Mark Rothko, Emperor Shi Huangdi (the builder of the Great Wall of China), Arturo Toscanini, Queen Victoria, Orson Welles, Walt Whitman, Andy Warhol.

RABBIT PEOPLE BORN IN THE...

Note: Western-calendar months are given as approximations only; to find a birth moon according to the Chinese lunisolar calendar, consult the chart on pp. 30–45.

FIRST MOON (FEBRUARY): These rabbits are born under the continuing strong influence of the previous Year of the Tiger, leading them to creative and bold action and a freedom that is unusual among rabbit people, making them excellent leaders in activities and business. They keep their aggressiveness and ambition quiet, but otherwise are very straightforward and open, with little patience for small details and small talk. They are successful people, loved and respected by their friends.

SECOND MOON (MARCH): Cautious and alert, they can be stubborn in resisting change, which may lead them into complacency and self-satisfaction. Apart from this, they share the good qualities of other rabbits, and are charming, active, clever, and confident; they are also excellent thinkers and talkers.

THIRD MOON (APRIL): These rabbits have the good luck of getting unexpected gifts in life. Impatient and emotional, they have less endurance than other rabbits, tend to keep moving on, and lead lives full of surprises. Their early years are quite uneven, but they have good energy and luck. Once focused, they can be very successful, with clear vision and insight.

FOURTH MOON (MAY): These lucky rabbits get constant attention, love, and caresses from others, and may be terribly spoiled. Always drawn to an outside attraction or an interesting possibility, they often switch careers or work two jobs at the same time—doing well in both. Highly gifted and resourceful, they shine in social activities.

FIFTH MOON (JUNE): Indecisive in thought and action, always worrying to the point of sleeplessness over the problems that confront them, they are as sensitive and curious as children, but dislike taking responsibility. They are gentle and warm, but enthusiastic only when they are not on the front line, or when someone is on the sideline protecting them. They are very interesting people to be with, and can be great friends for the sharing of feelings.

SIXTH MOON (JULY): Skillful but conservative, these rabbits are conformists who stick to middle-of-the-road approaches in the hope of pleasing everyone without taking an active position. Witty, sexy, and socially active, they are excellent partners for dinners and dances, but also enjoy good domestic environments, linens, flowers, and a solid home life.

SEVENTH MOON (AUGUST): These fighters and activists are the most ambitious and active of all the rabbit people. They love to talk and will debate with anyone they meet. Confident and persuasive, they often overdo it, causing difficult situations and hurt feelings for others, and may embarrass their friends in this way. They are creative trend-setters, who love fads and anything else that will stir up excitement and attract attention.

EIGHTH MOON (SEPTEMBER): These very interesting rabbits have double personalities formed by the yin-yang conflict between the spontaneous intuition of the Rabbit Year and the restraint of this month—hot and cold currents in continual alternation—and it takes quite a struggle to subdue them. Their lives are full of excitement and action. Their goals tend more toward artistic achievement than stability and career, achieved through the creative yin energy that stems from the restlessness of their internal subcurrents. They seem at times to be unstable and unfocused, but are nonetheless full of confidence in what they are doing.

NINTH MOON (OCTOBER): Thoughtful and sentimental, but also captivated by new ideas and trends, they enjoy being surrounded by both people and things. Many are collectors of art and other objects, sometimes to the point of obsession. Feelings are very important to them.

TENTH MOON (NOVEMBER): Reserved but friendly, always willing to compromise and to let others step forward first, they are polite, reasonable, and respectable. Many are oriented to the outdoors and to athletics, and all are concerned about their physical well-being. They are not loners, but busy social activity, noise, and night life are not to their liking; they prefer a quiet, private, lifestyle of peace and internal harmony.

ELEVENTH MOON (DECEMBER): These intelligent, individualistic rabbits are decisive persons who love to be different in thought and behavior, and are aggressive and stubborn in the skillful pursuit of what they want. Witty, naughty, and obsessive, they can deceive their best friends in pursuit of power and control.

TWELFTH MOON (JANUARY OF FOLLOWING YEAR): Born under the influence of the approaching Year of the Dragon, they are anxious to learn, get into action, and practice whatever they acquire without delay. They are likely to succeed when young. Artistic and creative, their idea of a good time may be arguing and debating with friends in contests of wit. They work hard, but like projects consisting of simple broad steps; detail and precision bore them. In a situation that requires complex thought they may simply fall asleep, or wander off in search of a simpler project.

THE LIFE CYCLE

HEALTH: Rabbit persons must pay attention to stomach and intestinal troubles, to which they are especially vulnerable. Their gentle and sensitive nature also makes them easily disturbed by abrupt environmental changes at home or at work. Noises, smoke, dirt, jostling, and strong light all upset their excellent ears, eyes, and noses and can make them ill.

MONEY: Most rabbit persons are conservative and careful in financial dealings, particularly skillful in long-term management planning, and excellent defensive players, with plenty of escape routes open. They will be wise to follow their natural inclination and avoid risk.

CAREER: Intelligent and able, with plenty of patience (yin energy) and a positive attitude, rabbits have a wide choice of careers, including art, education, engineering, business, finance, tourism and travel, health care and medicine, food-related occupations, and farming. They also thrive as art dealers, specialists in gems and precious metals, florists, performers, writers, politicians, and public relations consultants.

LOVE: In traditional Chinese folk belief, the rabbit is a fertility symbol, but this is only part of the story. Beautiful and charming, with big smiles that carry them far, rabbit people tend to be teasers rather than dedicated pursuers of passion. They are attractive, but gentle and somewhat passive; emotional but not passionate; romantic but very wide awake. It is characteristic of rabbits, both male and female, to be attracted to older admirers and pursuers, with the idea of being loved, cared for, treasured, and protected. Because their charm and wit are irresistible, romance comes to them very early in life.

RABBIT PARTNERS BORN IN
THE YEAR OF THE...

MOUSE: Mouse and rabbit share so many attitudes and traits that they are bound to be attracted to each other, but the mouse makes emotional demands that the rabbit may find difficult to meet. A long-term relationship works with great difficulty, and only if the limits are carefully defined beforehand.

OX: If the rabbit can get over feeling that the ox is a little too predictable, a relationship can be very satisfying, thanks to the ox's stability and weight, which can provide the reassurance the sensitive rabbit needs. A brief affair is going to be a bad experience for both parties, but a marriage, once the rabbit is convinced that it is the right thing, will be very solid and happy.

TIGER: The tiger is a hunter, and the rabbit rather enjoys being chased but not caught, so this is a relationship that can go nowhere for years and years. If the rabbit does eventually succumb, it may not be sorry; the strong and weak points of the pair complement each other, and the tiger, with someone calm and peaceful, may finally learn to behave!

RABBIT: Two rabbits together are an endless party; when they are not out on the town they are presenting one another with precious objects from their collections, telling each other outrageous anecdotes, or simply cuddling in front of the fire, with a glass and a snack close at hand. The relationship is, however, vulnerable to being broken up by third parties. One of the two will have to develop a territorial sense, or it may not last.

DRAGON: Dragon and rabbit both love to show off, and they dance to the same rhythm. They are even well-matched in their bad qualities. The rabbit may be a little nervous, watching the dragon's fancy steps, but it has its own power to keep the dragon guessing, and all will be well.

SNAKE: The snake has the ability to dominate the rabbit, tie it down, and eat it up; too often, in this relationship, the snake is perfectly contented while the rabbit suffers, longing to escape and at the same time unwilling to do so. Delicate young rabbits are cautioned not to let themselves be tied down too early.

HORSE: There are conflicts between rabbit and horse, but also many possibilities; most probably neither one takes the other very seriously, but they always have a good time together. They are always within reach of each other, and even if romance does not work out, they are likely to remain close friends.

RAM: In conflicts and conquests alike, the agile rabbit wins every time against the awkward ram, and may be tempted to gloat, feeling it has proved itself to be very tough and aggressive. This is a relationship with many ups and downs, though with real potential for true love. This enables the ram to swallow its frustrations, but only if the rabbit does its fair share of the giving.

MONKEY: Occasionally, rabbit finds monkey attractive, though too young and foolish for anything serious. Nevertheless, it can become serious, and the rabbit is in some danger of getting hurt, as it is vulnerable to the monkey's wicked tricks. Caution is advised, and some assertiveness.

ROOSTER: A star conflict makes this relationship a poor risk. In any case the picking and pecking at all hours of the noisy rooster is hard for the quiet rabbit to bear, so it rarely seems a risk worth taking.

DOG: A relationship that requires some work; the dog tends to be at fault, making excessive demands, but it is the rabbit that must pay the price, becoming more and more nervous unless things begin to change. The work has a reward, though; after the early stages this is a very happy, stable romance.

PIG: Pig and rabbit can have a lot of fun together, and are certain to be good friends. Romance may be another matter, and if it doesn't work out, the rabbit may have to take much of the blame, since it is misses the sense of drama and tension that other lovers provide and decides to create a little tension in its own right.

THE YEAR OF THE DRAGON

CHEN

DRAGON YEARS

1904	February 16 to February 3, 1905
1916	February 4 to January 22, 1917
1928	January 23 to February 9, 1929
1940	February 8 to January 26, 1941
1952	January 27 to February 13, 1953
1964	February 13 to February 1, 1965
1976	January 31 to February 17, 1977
1988	February 17 to February 5, 1989
2000	February 5 to January 23, 2001
2012	January 23 to February 9, 2013
2024	February 10 to January 28, 2025
2036	January 28 to February 14, 2037
2048	February 14 to February 1, 2049

ASSOCIATIONS

EARTHLY BRANCH CHARACTER: *Chen* is a yang character, but is said to be a pictorial representation of a woman bending forward in embarrassment, probably at the time of her monthly period, and hence denotes a period or division of time. The woman does not conceive at this time, but knows that she may do so soon—similarly, any period of time may be said to carry latent potential, and this character is associated with time, surprises, and auspicious events, and by extension with activity, vitality, and prosperity.

The essence of those born in this year is unpredictability. They are strong, brilliant, and mysterious, with no one knowing what they will do next, except that it is likely to be something magnificent. They arouse excitement and admiration wherever they go, and are usually blessed with good luck, though their instability can make them unhappy and hamper their careers.

ANIMAL: The dragon *(long)*, unlike the other animals of the Chinese zodiac, is a mythical beast. Unlike the evil, monstrous dragons of Western mythology, Chinese dragons are beneficent if unreliable creatures who live in the heavens and command the wind, mist, rain, thunder, and lightning that make the farmers' crops grow on earth below. Thus the peasants, who lived in constant hope and fear of rain, drought, and flooding, felt they knew the dragon's character and habits as well as those of any of the other animals.

Dragons are capable of protean transformations, assuming any form they choose. Those born in the Year of the Dragon are whimsical and extravagant, full of new ideas and bursts of energy, and have extraordinary power to influence the outcome of any situation, though it is never clear in advance whether they will do so or not. It is not wise to depend on them too much, but often unavoidable, because they love to be at the center of everything, and generally establish themselves there. They possess great talents in the creative and active realms, and if they deliver on their promise all will be well.

ORDER: The dragon occupies the fifth position in the Chinese zodiac, a powerful and radiant position of reverence and mystery. It is associated with the Chinese emperor, whose honor, mystery, benevolence, and power to guide the country and protect the people from evil spirits are symbolized in art by the five-clawed imperial dragon. Dragon people are ambitious and adventurous in character, always planning for unexpected events, and their talents match their ambitions. Strong and magnetic in personality, they are capable of being great leaders in any field.

ELEMENT: Of the five Chinese elements, Earth is assigned to the dragon. Earth gives birth to Metal, conflicts with Water, overcomes Fire and is subject to Wood; it is wise for those born in this year to invest in land, minerals, and plants. The dragon draws its great strength from the earth, but makes its home among the water-bearing clouds, from which it brings prosperity to those below, but not necessarily to itself. Its greatest weaknesses, instability and a lack of realism, come directly out of this disconnectedness.

STAR GROUP: The Metal Star (Venus) rules the Palace of the Year of the Dragon , which houses three Lodges: Yi, Zhen, and Jiao, corresponding to stars within Crater, Hydra, Corvus, Spica and Virgo. There is said to be potential for major conflict with those born in the Year of the Dog; otherwise, few dare to quarrel with the clever and aggressive dragon, but dragons supply themselves with more than enough conflicts to keep them busy. It is easy for them to draw support from all types of people through their charm and good humor, but they are sometimes too independent-minded to realize this.

FAVORABLE DIRECTION: East by southeast. Projects, plans, and moves oriented a third of the way south from due east will be profitable. Traveling in China, those born in this year will enjoy best of all the beautiful canal-interlaced landscapes around Suzhou and the lovely town itself, as well as the remarkable night life of Shanghai.

FAVORABLE MONTH: Mid-May to mid-June, the most vibrant and prosperous months of the year, when flowers bloom and leaves stretch out beyond the tips of the twigs. On the fifth day of the lunar month, all China celebrates the Patriotic Poet's Festival, in commemoration of the great poet Chu Yuan of the Warring States Period, 3rd century B C, who drowned himself in grief over the corruption of the state. On this day, teams of young men run fierce rowing races in their magnificently accoutered dragon boats and everyone eats glutinous-rice dumplings wrapped in bamboo leaves. The transformation of the earth matches a transformation in the hearts of dragon people, when serious thought and action unite for a breakthrough into closer contact with things.

FAVORABLE HOUR: 7:00 AM to 9:00 AM, the busy beginning hours of the day, when the yang force, still a little unsteady but awesomely powerful, rises and makes transformations. Each day is a new day, a new page in the diary, a new step toward an idea or project, and dragon people greet it at the peak of their strength, deciding on which of their many possible identities they should live in for the next twenty-four hours.

FAVORABLE NUMBERS: 3, 4, 5, 6, 15, 21, 34, 35, 36, 45.

THE WHOLE PERSON

CHARACTER: Youthful, optimistic, and ambitious, brave and aggressive in action—those born in the Year of the Dragon are full of yang energy to get things moving. They also have plenty of practical ability, despite the whimsical way they present themselves. They enjoy starting new things and being in command of them, in full control and at ease, like an emperor holding audience at court. With their powerful iron claws and spiky sweeping tails, they can eliminate obstacles in battle after battle until they achieve victory.

Dragon people can be witty and funny, open and generous to friends, though their tempers are hot. They are honorable people, always met with respect. Endowed with unequalled creative forces, they are often very physically attractive. Delighted to be at the center of attention, they may be incautious and intense—they are not easy to tame. They are very sensitive to changes in natural environment, and supporters of environmental causes; they consider themselves the "sons and daughters of heaven" and are therefore the protectors of this heritage and legacy.

EMOTIONS: Underlying the dragon robes and yang energy are currents of insecurity and nervousness. Endless internal struggles with fear and success, hot and cold, fill the air with uncertainty and the sense that the unexpected is about to happen. But after a time trapped in cloud and mist or exploding with thunder and lightning, the rainbow comes through and the dragon performs its magnificent dance once again.

Dragon people love the outdoors and nature, their second home and preferred playground. They are not home-oriented, but they expect the home and family to be oriented to them, and regard them positively and protectively. They can err on the side of overprotectiveness, but it is good to have a dragon bodyguard in a time of crisis.

WEAKNESSES: The worst situation for a dragon is to be trapped in a small muddy pond with little room to maneuver. There the dragon will suffer and become disillusioned, roaring to free itself from confinement and take off toward the open sky. With their ferocious tempers, it is wise for them to make a special effort toward balance and harmony in the continuous flow and flux of the life force, and to avoid extremism and fanaticism, or it may be hard to keep their imperial crowns on their heads.

LIFESTYLE: Often highly status-conscious, dragons are good at showing off and trying new trends and fashionable things. They are healthy eaters, enjoying good food and drink; they tend not to be consistent with only one kind of cuisine, because they are active and restless. They love anything beautiful and are not afraid of getting attention and attracting controversy. They are free spenders and active participants in life, who enjoy physical pleasures, exercise, travel, parties, cars, the arts, and so on. Many play a successful role organizing their communities, with charm and power.

FAMOUS DRAGON PEOPLE: Susan B. Anthony, George Balanchine, Pearl Buck, Lewis Carroll, Salvador Dali, Sigmund Freud, Cary Grant, J. Paul Getty, Immanuel Kant, Willem de Kooning, John Lennon, Eduard Monet, Friedrich Nietzsche, Yehudi Menuhin, Florence Nightingale, Jean-Jacques Rousseau, Bernard Shaw, Mae West, Woodrow Wilson.

DRAGON PEOPLE BORN IN THE...

Note: Western-calendar months are given as approximations only; to find a birth moon according to the Chinese lunisolar calendar, consult the chart on pp. 30–45.

FIRST MOON (FEBRUARY): Optimistic and emotional, they are as capable of being practical as other dragons but more thoughtful and intellectual. They always come up with unconventional ideas and points of view, and carry a mysterious aura that keeps others guessing, making it hard to understand or know them.

SECOND MOON (MARCH): Underneath, their egos and ambitions are at the boil, ready to explode at any moment, but they maintain a surface sensitivity and gentleness that makes them seem different from other dragons. They are quietly powerful and aggressive, aiming at winning above anything else. The gentle behavior of these dragons is a great weapon for gaining respect and success from friends and enemies alike.

THIRD MOON (APRIL): Physically strong, optimistic, and outgoing, they can be noisy and overdo self-expression. They are big spenders and love showy things; aggressively, competitively, with wit and boldness, they pursue what they want, not easily discouraged by obstacles. They are remarkably resilient and alive, always warm, helpful, friendly and open, and their lives are full of colorful events.

FOURTH MOON (MAY): Old yin energy balances their character, adding to their power a consistency other dragons lack. They are always in charge of groups, loved by friends for their matchless enthusiasm and daring and feared by enemies for their hot temper. They are upfront, confrontational, and strongly opinionated, and they love material possessions and fantasies.

FIFTH MOON (JUNE): Intense and concentrated in work and action, dangerous to cross. In this month, dragons are at the peak of their power, commanding the mists, clouds, rains and thunderings of the sky, and a midsummer night storm is something one always remembers. Brave in pursuing their ideas and unafraid of self-sacrifice and suffering on the way to their goals, they can run into severe ups and downs in their lives, but will eventually overcome with faith and strength.

SIXTH MOON (JULY): The most sensitive and artistic dragons, they are thinkers and intellectuals, fine writers and critics, skillful debaters and talkers, with an aura that keeps you waiting and then shocks you with surprises. But in action, as opposed to talk, they are gentle with others, especially those close to them, caring, and concerned.

SEVENTH MOON (AUGUST): Creative and active, with great ability to win confidence from those around them, many are very inventive, persistent, and successful in pursuing what they want. They are warm and generous, with a good sense of humor, and quite forgiving to those who cross them.

EIGHTH MOON (SEPTEMBER): Practical people, good at detail and planning, these dragons do whatever they do for a reason, usually connected with material gain and the quest for money and power. Very manipulative and status-conscious, they care a lot about who their friends are and work hard to impress others. They are not the type to endure poverty and suffering, and will act to do something about it.

NINTH MOON (OCTOBER): Courageous and brainy, active and witty, intelligent but absent-minded, and even naughty like children, they can be very creative and eccentric. They are certainly not loners, but in romance, as opposed to friendship, they can sometimes be unfaithful and irresponsible. They may not intend to hurt others, but are acting out their own fantasies and daydreams, and when they awaken it may be too late.

TENTH MOON (NOVEMBER): These are unusual people, quiet and passive like hidden dragons at rest, who will surprise everyone when the right moment arrives by what they can do and achieve. Their inner strength and potential are remarkable. They can be socially eccentric and perhaps loners, but they are not unfriendly. They are not always easy to understand, however: like tidal waves, their high and low points mask the consistency of the underlying force.

ELEVENTH MOON (DECEMBER): Warriors and determined people, they are childlike in their attitude toward life as a game to be won. They are also childlike in the naughty pleasure they take in fights and arguments. While friends may get annoyed, they won't take it too seriously, and will laugh and love them all the same. These dragons pursue what they want with optimism, impatient with delays. Unpredictable but goodhearted and very interesting, they are free spirits, always their own bosses.

TWELFTH MOON (JANUARY OF FOLLOWING YEAR): Somewhat detached and cold on the outside, under the influence of the coming Year of the Snake, they are warm and active inside. They are informal but cautious, not as fond of crowds as other dragon people, but friendly and helpful once you get to know them. Many are very successful professionals, and they enjoy family life as well as solitude.

THE LIFE CYCLE

HEALTH: In general dragons are physically healthier than most people, but need to pay attention to dangers relating to stress and the internal struggle of hot and cold tempers—abuse of self and others, addictions of various kinds, and even serious cases of depression and bipolar affective disorder. They will do best taking a philosophical attitude, listening and watching the river flow according to its own course and level rather than putting themselves at the mercy of their emotions. With effort and a positive attitude, they have a unique ability for self-transcendence into balance and harmony that should help them protect themselves from these problems.

MONEY: Their combination of intelligence, ambition, and good luck makes dragons skillful in finance and management. They are aggressive conservatives, long-term defensive planners. Although they love to spend money they are good at making it as well, and always on the lookout for new trends and movements. Their enjoyment of nature and the outdoors leads them to excel in dealings related to water, air, earth, plants, minerals, and natural resources.

CAREER: With their positive energy and intelligence, the sky is the limit for dragons as far as career is concerned. They can fit into almost any field. Some particularly apt possibilities are public relations, politics, visual arts, communications, international trade, transportation, and shipping. They make fine athletes, artists, engineers, financial managers, environmental experts, lawyers, travel agents, geologists and gem experts, housing developers, jewelers, and space and marine scientists.

LOVE: Dragon people need lots of friends and lots of love. Intense and possessive in romance, they are at the same time somewhat doubtful and reserved. The mixture of different currents makes their love stories magnificently dramatic, but they have plenty of yang energy to keep the love boat afloat among the clouds, mists, and rain—as well as the occasional thunderstorm—that are part of their normal environment.

DRAGON PARTNERS BORN IN
THE YEAR OF THE...

MOUSE: Full of contrast, but united by their love of fun, mouse and dragon share many active and happy moments, partying and exploring exotic foods and cultures together. They are also well matched in less attractive qualities, each always withholding something from the other. If this causes problems, dragon can help by understanding that it is just as guilty as mouse.

OX: The ox's stubborn strength pitted against the dragon's mercurial power means that conflict is inevitable, and very hard to work out. This is an upsetting, exhausting relationship, but dragon may want to make an effort to hold on to it, and it could be the right choice for the very long run.

TIGER: These two different kinds of yang strength can complement each other. Friends never expect the relationship to endure, but it probably will, and very happily—dragon and tiger make few demands on one another, but those they do are almost always satisfied.

RABBIT: This relationship is harmonious and productive for both partners; the rabbit enjoys the dragon's surprises and the dragon appreciates the rabbit's calm. They compensate for one another's defects and admire one another's strengths.

DRAGON: This is an extreme relationship, good or bad. Each dragon loves to be at the center of everything, and it's not easy to make room for another dragon at the center of your life. If you can do it, it can be really glorious, with each spurring the other to ever greater heights.

SNAKE: Dragon and snake can be best friends, but a romantic relationship may not work, for one apparently trivial reason or another. The dragon may not try very hard to make it work, which the snake finds offputting; if they must drift apart they must, and the separation may as well be amicable, so that losing a lover does not mean losing a friend as well.

HORSE: This is a relationship fraught with difficulties. The straightforward horse finds dragon devious rather than whimsical, and doesn't often care to examine its own feelings more closely. Physical compatibility keeps them going for a while, but it will take much work to make it into something deeper.

RAM: Although they are very different people, dragon sees all of ram's good qualities and wants badly to build a strong relationship, but ram is likely to be somewhat frightened by dragon's mercurial temperament and shy away. It is very strongly attracted, however, and will stop resisting if the dragon can exert some self-discipline and make compromises.

MONKEY: The dragon has the rare ability to make the naughty monkey behave with respect. The monkey benefits from the resulting maturity, and the dragon has a wonderful time with its clever new friend. This relationship will not be free of conflict, but when it is good it is very good.

ROOSTER: The dragon sees the rooster as a phoenix, a glorious mate; they are deeply attracted to each other and always look good together. Problems arise because the rooster is unwilling to accept the happiness it finds in this relationship, and keeps looking for reasons to feel suspicious. The dragon needs to be patient; the problems are not permanent.

DOG: A relationship between these two volcanoes waiting to explode is full of risks. Any romance will be rough sailing indeed, and the dragon can really get hurt.

PIG: The dragon doesn't mind staying at home in this comfortable, funny, and almost conflict-free relationship, which seems to work by itself without much effort. The pig enjoys it too, though it will get a little nervous at times. No need to worry, but effort in any relationship is required, and dragon still has to do its part.

THE YEAR
OF THE
SNAKE

SI

SNAKE YEARS

1905	February 4 to January 24, 1906
1917	January 23 to February 10, 1918
1929	February 10 to January 29, 1930
1941	January 27 to February 14, 1942
1953	February 14 to February 2, 1954
1965	February 2 to January 20, 1966
1977	February 18 to February 6, 1978
1989	February 6 to January 26, 1990
2001	January 24 to February 11, 2002
2013	February 10 to January 30, 2014
2025	January 29 to February 16, 2026
2037	February 15 to February 3, 2038
2049	February 2 to January 22, 2050

ASSOCIATIONS

EARTHLY BRANCH CHARACTER: *Si* is a picture of the fetus within the womb, and as the child is already becoming a new entity distinct from its parents, this character denotes an action that differentiates or distinguishes—by extension one that causes the actor to excel, and to come to a new horizon with a surplus of good energy. The essence of those born in the Year of the Snake is gathered strength, the quiet accumulation of energy that will serve to distinguish the person. They are enduring, patient, passively aggressive, calculating, conservative and quietly powerful, always ready when the time comes to make their mark.

ANIMAL: The snake *(she)* is a wise reptile symbolizing fertility in Chinese folklore, a creature that draws great reserves of yin energy from its closeness to mother earth. Chinese myths are full of stories associating snakes with female deities who charm or bewitch scholarly young men and give birth to super-gifted children who become leaders in royal courts. These snake-goddesses are heroines, adepts of literature and the martial arts, or benevolent goddesses who dare to steal sacred medicine from the heavenly palace of the Jade Emperor to save the lives of the sick and poor in times of plague and disaster.

The snake seems quiet and slow but is alert, intelligent, strong-minded, and potentially dangerous, ready to strike suddenly. People born in the Year of the Snake are intellectuals, apparently passive, making their plans coolly and carefully in anticipation of the decisive moment. They may seem cold and somewhat self-involved, but this is partly the result of an iron self-control. They are deeply caring once they have made a serious commitment, work hard without showing the effort, and are very difficult to defeat once they are ready to move.

ORDER: The Snake occupies the sixth position in the Chinese zodiac, which draws its importance from its centrality. Snakes are remarkable people who wait with endurance and strength in the center of vibrancy and activity. They are less likely to occupy official leadership positions than to be in control behind the scenes, which they prefer as it enables them to maintain their privacy. But if the right moment comes they will not hesitate to assert themselves publicly, and attain the highest goals.

ELEMENT: Of the five Chinese elements, Fire is assigned to the Year of the Snake, in conflict with Water, overcoming Metal, supported by Wood and in complementary relation with Earth. The Fire associations extend to interests in energy, power, and action, and snake persons can make profitable investments in ventures relating to the conquering of metal and minerals. They draw strength from everything they come in contact with, gradually growing in power. Their chief weakness is sometimes to wait too long, until every circumstance is exactly right, giving competitors a chance to gain the advantage.

STAR GROUP: The Water Star (Mercury) rules the Palace of the Year of the Snake, which houses three Lodges or Star-Spirits: Xing, Zhang, and Yi, corresponding to stars within Hydra and Crater. There is potential for serious conflict with those born in the Year of the Pig. On the whole, snake people avoid conflict, hoping to see their enemies destroy themselves through some impetuous, unprepared move, while they build up their own support networks through carefully calibrated favors.

FAVORABLE DIRECTION: South by southeast. The projects and excursions of snake people will prosper if they are oriented in a direction one third eastward from due south, the most fertile, sunny, and prosperous point on the compass. Traveling in China, they should restrict themselves to places with fine, predictable weather, and will have the happiest time in the favorite city of scholars and poets, the Southern Song capital of Hangzhou.

FAVORABLE MONTH: Mid-June to mid-July, the hot, bright, sunny time of the year when animals, insects, and plants are in full activity and growth, and snakes prepare and wait for their prey, alert and watching everything that moves, ready for profit and gain. Snake people should be happy because it is a serious time for taking action, and they are already testing out ideas and energy for projects and the fulfillment of private desires.

FAVORABLE HOUR: The *Si* hour, from 9:00 AM to 11:00 AM, is the time when the yang power has fully gathered its strength and the working day begins. Snakes are late risers, not fully awake until the sun is completely risen, absorbing its warmth before they are ready for action. Thus snake people tend to be at their best in midmorning, well-prepared for action and productivity, new growth and auspicious moves.

FAVORABLE NUMBERS: 1, 2, 4, 6, 13, 24, 42, 46.

THE WHOLE PERSON

CHARACTER: Those born in the Year of the Snake are usually quiet, slow, even passive in appearance. But on the inside they are full of fire, vibrant and active, interested in growth, the exploration of new developments in business and investment, creative work, and love and romance. Those who try to take advantage of them will regret it; snake people are especially efficient and hardworking, and have a great ability both to manipulate and to endure, patiently working toward their goals. They are more in control than they often seem to be, deep thinkers and intellectuals, cautious and skeptical, whose instinctive and incisive judgments and insights have unusual power.

EMOTIONS: Snake people keep their emotions and ambitions well hidden, guarding their privacy, and since they do not care much about showing off to others to get attention, they are often misunderstood as being detached and cool. But in reality they are warm and friendly, with a delicate sensitivity to others. Long-distance travel and frequent moving upset them. They prefer home to drifting around the world, and are good home-makers and providers, deeply attached to children and other family members.

WEAKNESSES: The snake person's attitude toward life is more intellectual than physical, but they are very sentimental and their mental health can be delicate. Upsetting mood changes can break their concentration and disturb their overall balance in life. Companionship, moral support, and love are needed as a source of energy and power to overcome this.

LIFESTYLE: Very artistic and creative, snake people love entertainment and culture, especially music and dance. They are quite social, party-goers who are often found at movies, the theater, concerts, art galleries, and museums. They are conservative in matters of taste as in other respects, and will not be the first jump into something, preferring to wait and see. Uninterested in display for its own sake or for prestige, they are not big spenders. Because they are oversensitive to weather and environment, they may like outdoor activities but will generally prefer the controlled comforts of indoor life, and snacking on little crunchy sweet things.

FAMOUS SNAKE PEOPLE: Joan Baez, Johannes Brahms, Copernicus, Charles Darwin, Bob Dylan, Mahatma Gandhi, Martha Graham, Greta Garbo, John F. Kennedy, Martin Luther King, Jr., Abraham Lincoln, Mao Zedong, Henri Matisse, Felix Mendelssohn, Joan Miro, Jacqueline Onassis, Thomas Paine, Pablo Picasso, and Franz Schubert.

SNAKE PEOPLE BORN IN THE...

Note: Western-calendar months are given as approximations only; to find a birth moon according to the Chinese lunisolar calendar, consult the chart on pp. 30–45.

FIRST MOON (FEBRUARY): These articulate, possessive snakes are talented, creative, temperamental and not shy about expressing their likes and dislikes. They are prone to depression, loneliness, and boredom. They love to collect things, including objects they have made themselves. If they can teach themselves patience they will be successful at an early age, because they are intense and productive workers as long as they are not bored. Their urge to spend money, untypical of snake people, gives them trouble with budgeting, and they are easily discouraged in affairs of the heart when things do not go their way.

SECOND MOON (MARCH): Skeptics and doubters who like to keep things to themselves, snakes born in this month are also very intelligent, decisive, and alert. More concerned with inner growth and spirituality than material wealth, they hold tightly to ideals and high standards, and expend much yin energy trying to find the reasons behind things.

THIRD MOON (APRIL): Ambitious characters who often start and run their own businesses, they love to be bosses or managers with authority and personal freedom. Competent and capable in whatever they do, their weaknesses are overconfidence and aggression, through which they may hurt those close to them. If they cultivate a good sense of humor, and sit back and laugh at life, they will be as well loved as they are successful.

FOURTH MOON (MAY): Though they appear to be the most passive of snakes, overly self-centered and preferring the shade to the limelight, on the inside they are especially strong minded, ambitious, passionate, and emotional, and must guard against all kinds of addictions. They are good plotters and planners, but to achieve harmony in life they need to work at maintaining a balanced perspective.

FIFTH MOON (JUNE): Cleverer and wittier than most snakes, fond of buying beautiful things, their personalities can carry them to extremes of activity or inactivity, earliness or lateness, strength or weakness, and so on. But their apparent indecisiveness and occasionally annoying behavior are the expression of artistic, searching minds that need to be given extra time and space to stretch out in.

SIXTH MOON (JULY): Especially slow, alert, cautious and trustworthy, these snakes have great sensitivity and understanding for others that often bring them success as business executives and managers. They are especially sensitive to scents and cleanliness, preoccupied with baths, massages and skin care, and take great pride in clean clothes and environments, polished cutlery and scrubbed floors.

SEVENTH MOON (AUGUST): Snake people born in the powerful yang heat of this month are sensitive and restless, more likely to go out looking for action than other snakes. Internal struggles and indecision, as well as external stress, cause them problems, but they always find their way out of a dilemma. Normally very attractive physically, they are good at getting others to help them, especially when young.

EIGHTH MOON (SEPTEMBER): Aggressive and troublesome in some respects, which makes them good warriors, but also highly responsible homemakers. They can be very overconfident, and it is likely that a crisis in mid-stream will shock and depress them. Friends and helping hands are important, and they should remember that building bridges is more challenging than burning them down.

NINTH MOON (OCTOBER): Optimistic, playful, and funny, with a youthful outlook, they can be misunderstood by friends as easy going and unfocused, but despite appearances they are capable people. They are more overtly sociable than most snakes, in the outgoing spirit of this month. Their friendliness is as sincere as it looks.

TENTH MOON (NOVEMBER): Thinkers who suffer from the conflicting influences of hot and cold currents, they long to let go and enjoy themselves in a crowd, but tend to withdraw in the thick of socializing to be alone with their thoughts. They are creative and outspoken, with independent and often controversial ideas, but are also possessive, jealous, and on the self-centered side. They often express their conflicts by being changeable and unpredictable.

ELEVENTH MOON (DECEMBER): Open and straightforward, friendly and passionate, they are good friends and faithful to their families. It is even more of a mistake than with other snake people to treat them as passive and low-key. They are fond of good food and parties and make good organizers and managers, with excellent communication skills and a fine instinct for beauty and design.

TWELFTH MOON (JANUARY OF FOLLOWING YEAR): Under the influence of the coming Year of the Horse, they are open and direct. Temporary obstacles will not deter them from trying again and again to achieve the goal. Stubborn, obsessive, and regimented, it takes them some time to gain the flexibility of attitude they need for success.

THE LIFE CYCLE

HEALTH: Snake people are more sensitive to changes in weather and environment than most, and vulnerable to illnesses caused by extremes of hot and cold. They love to sleep and need plenty of it, so a resting and relaxing environment is important to them. Excess of any kind is bad for them, whether it be overindulgence food, alcohol, and drugs or simply too much stress. Fortunately they are wise and know their territory well; they are health-conscious and very careful about their lifestyle on the whole, and have few serious health problems as long as they are in control.

MONEY: In finance as elsewhere, snake persons observe cautiously and patiently from the sidelines, awaiting the correct moment for making their move. They are conservative and defensive in the money game, loving ownership but not fond of spending, and are too wise to rise to the bait of an attractive but unsound risk. Particular profitability is indicated for projects relating to plants and land and especially anything to do with the conquest of metal, because of the associated Fire element.

CAREER: Hardworking, intelligent, quiet and patient, snakes do well in many kinds of work, especially anything related to mind, thoughts, words, sounds, and movements. Their ability for creative thought helps them to go far in their chosen careers. They succeed in arts and crafts, design, education, environment-related professions, financial management and careers, businesses related to land or real estate, scientific research and technology, visual and other communications, politics and public relations, and as dancers, geologists, gem experts, lawyers, health professionals, and musicians.

LOVE: The snake is a fertility symbol in Chinese mythology, and snake persons are sexy, passionate, and warm, making charming, though passive, lovers. They are often clever teasers as well. When they are in love, which is all the time, they can become possessive and obsessed. It is dangerous to cross them, because they are skillful plotters, and a snakebite can be a painful surprise! At the same time, they do not always remain focused on one love object for long, and are prone to infidelity. Thus the very thing the romantic snakes want and need is difficult to maintain and keep; the closer to their desire they seem to be, the further away from it they really are. Energy and patience will help them bring it to fruition in the end.

SNAKE PARTNERS BORN IN THE YEAR OF THE...

MOUSE: The snake can eat a mouse for breakfast without even thinking about it, and may regard this relationship as a casual amusement. Mouse and snake share many common interests and purposes, but neither will get much happiness out of this romance unless the snake is making a real commitment.

OX: Ox and snake are both possessive, and neither likes to make the first move. If they get together, they will have to know how to behave, define their boundaries and limits, and keep their word; if they manage to do this, they can be happy together.

TIGER: The flashy, noble tiger seems an odd character to the snake, not necessarily attractive. But, being passive, it may give in to the tiger's seduction, and then both have a rough time in store: conflicts and fights, followed most likely by mutual betrayal and separation.

RABBIT: As a rule, the gentle rabbit suffers in a relationship with the snake. Occasionally, though, the rabbit brings out the deeper side of the snake, not the flighty romantic side but the conservatism and delicate understanding of the needs of others. In this case everything can be fine, but otherwise snake should really keep a distance and avoid causing pain.

DRAGON: Dragon and snake make a fun couple, although the snake may need to ask whether its demands are not a little too heavy. There is great potential for happiness, although making it last may require some adjustments.

SNAKE: Two snakes may have some trouble, with each expecting the other to be the dominant partner, but they have many advantages in learning to love and tolerate one another, and may end up sharing a nest, laying dozens of little eggs.

HORSE: The horse is always outdoors, looking after some new distraction, while the snake is inside waiting for some attention. There are no smooth paths in this romance, but it is worth a try, because there is much mutual respect and physical attraction to build on. Guard against infidelity.

RAM: Each finds the other too cold, and there may be many hurt feelings and miscommunications. Happiness is not impossible, however, and the snake becomes a better person for making the effort.

MONKEY: Many snakes feel at home in the trees where the monkeys play, and they are just as clever and tricky, though different in style. This is a dangerous relationship, full of game-playing, and not likely to last long, but full of educational entertainment for both sides as long as it does.

ROOSTER: One of those relationships that seems impossible from the start. The rooster, with its conceit and fussiness, manages to make the normally calm snake irritable and quarrelsome. All the fuss is only on the surface, however. Beneath, they may be building a solid relationship that will last.

DOG: Snake and dog can be great friends, enjoying each other's company. For a deeper relationship, the snake must learn not to be too possessive, giving the dog room to bark, jump, and run. Mutual attraction makes this not so hard to achieve.

PIG: A deeply conflicted, star-crossed relationship. Since it is almost impossible for the pig to understand what is going on in that deep snake mind, or for the snake to appreciate the pig's joyous humane qualities, it is probably better not to try.

THE YEAR OF THE HORSE

WU

HORSE YEARS

1906	January 25 to February 12, 1907
1918	February 11 to January 31, 1919
1930	January 30 to February 16, 1931
1942	February 15 to February 4, 1943
1954	February 3 to January 23, 1955
1966	January 21 to February 8, 1967
1978	February 7 to January 27, 1979
1990	January 27 to February 14, 1991
2002	February 12 to January 31, 2003
2014	January 31 to February 18, 2015
2026	February 17 to February 5, 2027
2038	February 4 to January 25, 2039
2050	January 23 to February 10, 2051

ASSOCIATIONS

EARTHLY BRANCH CHARACTER: *Wu*, representing a pestle, originally denoted the acts of hitting or offending; but its secondary sense, denoting a stepping stone, an intersection, or the midpoint of a sequence, has been dominant for many millennia. The Year of the Horse, coming at the center of the twelve-year cycle, has often been a historical turning point, as for example in the First World War (1918), the Great Depression (1930), the Second World War (1942), and the Cultural Revolution in China (1966). The essence of those born in this year is to be decisive; they are born leaders, eager to help out others in time of need and crisis. They are also artistically active, friendly, intelligent, and beautiful.

ANIMAL: In Chinese mythology, the horse is paired with the dragon as a joint symbol of spirit, vitality, power, and good luck. Horses were honored and loved in traditional China, and emperors enthusiastically bred and raised them in the imperial stables, especially during the Tang Dynasty (AD 618–905), when they were a favorite subject for artists, and when the game of polo was invented. The emperors used to award a white horse as a mark of special favor to those who had achieved the highest honor, and even now the folk expression "white horse" is used to describe a handsome and pure young scholar of high attainments.

The horse *(ma)* is an energetic, clever, and swift animal. People born in this year are forceful and bold in actions, moving quickly and confidently. They are offensive players with strength and intelligence, who advance ambitiously toward new positions in business, investments, and romance. They are brave and straightforward in communicating their likes and desires. Honorable and social, they dearly love cultural pursuits and enjoy all kinds of oratory, debate, and ordinary conversation.

ORDER: The seventh position, at the center of the Chinese zodiac, is the most youthful and active of all the positions, energetic, radiant, and vibrant. There is a folk prejudice concerning this with reference to the years 1846, 1906, 1966, 2026, etc., which are Fire Horse (*yan ma*) years, in the forty-third year of the grand sixty-year cycle. Some less sophisticated astrologers regard people born in these years as catastrophically destructive, because of the use of the term *yan* ("double fire" or"blazing") instead of *huo* ("fire" in the ordinary sense). However, the Fire Horse year is simply the greatest turning point of all. Turning points present not only danger but also opportunity, and opportunity is what people born in the Year of the Horse are quick to seize.

ELEMENT: Of the five Chinese elements, Fire is assigned to the Year of the Horse, in conflict with Metal and complemented by Wood and Earth. Water can destroy Fire as Fire can evaporate Water, and there is a potential for major conflict with those born in the Water-dominated Year of the Mouse. The strengths of those born in the Year of the Horse are nourished in the same way as Fire, by the air, and they are at their most effective in the open spaces where they have plenty of room to maneuver. Their weaknesses are evident in situations of standoff, where neither aggression nor retreat is an option, and they may succumb to depression and lassitude.

STAR GROUP: The Sun is the "planet" ruling the Palace of the Year of the Horse, which houses four Lodges or Star-Spirits: Jing, Gui, Liu, and Xing, corresponding to stars in Gemini, Cancer, and Hydra. Horse people run headlong into much conflict in their lives, striking out against whatever they see as unjust and wrong; they receive support from many friends who admire them and adopt their causes. They are not normally good at working alone, and tend to be front players who leave the detail work for others to complete, freeing them to charge forward into combat, protecting their comrades or loved ones.

FAVORABLE DIRECTION: South, the home of the Red Firebird or Phoenix, a divine bird who dwells in the Vermilion Hills, appearing in the empire only at the rare times when reason prevails. Her element is Fire, and she governs the summer. As a symbol of sun, warmth, and prosperity, she makes a splendid guardian spirit for those born in the Year of the Horse, who share her love for justice throughout the land. At a more commonplace level, horses do well to orient their plans and projects in a southerly direction, and traveling in China, they should not fail to gallop through the open delta country of the Pearl River in Guangdong and sample the classical cuisine of Guangzhou and Hongkong.

FAVORABLE MONTH: Mid-July to mid-August, the period at mid-year when animals, insects and plants are at the peak of their growth before the autumnal decline begins. Horses run freely through the fields and the woods, expressing their energy without fear of being bogged down in mud, because this is when the whole earth is as dry as a race course. This is the time when horse people should make their major life decisions, at the turning point of the year. In the Chinese religious calendar, it is the so-called month of the "Hungry Ghosts," when the community holds a festival to make offerings to the spirits of dead souls unfortunate enough not to be venerated by their descendants at family altars.

FAVORABLE HOUR: 11:00 AM to 1:00 PM, the midday, when the sun is hottest and brightest, and the yang force is at its peak, providing strength and vitality to the whole earth. It is also lunchtime, of course, when humans refresh themselves after a hard morning's work, and perhaps stretch out under a tree, away from the sun, for a siesta. Horse persons may not want to linger—their favorite meal is at the dinner hour in any case; they can cope with any amount of sunshine and put this time, when everyone else is relatively inactive, to practical use.

FAVORABLE NUMBERS: 1, 3, 4, 8, 13, 14, 34, 41, 43.

THE WHOLE PERSON

CHARACTER: Horse people are aggressive and ambitious, capable of employing any means to achieve an objective. They seem self-centered, but this is hard to judge, because they can be extremely generous as well, and active participants in whatever they get involved in, whether a job or a party. Constantly busy people, with skillful hands and minds, they are often found practicing handicrafts or cooking exotic cuisines. It is important for them to have a stable environment in which they can move freely, and plenty of tender loving care.

EMOTIONS: Although they may be great money makers, creative leaders, or successful in other ways, horse people value freedom above everything else. They can be very impatient, irritated by wear and tear, and infuriated by teasing that goes beyond certain limits. Then they react with a temper as hot as the noonday sun; or else they choose not to fight, since they have too much pride to allow themselves to be dragged through the mud. They may simply walk out on a situation without explanation or notice, wanting a better deal or no deal at all.

WEAKNESSES: People born in this year pay little attention to insincere praise, unrealistic offers, impossible lovers, and mighty powers that would like to eat them alive. Their dangers come from their own characters: a potential lack of focus, readiness to be distracted, unwillingness to endure a situation in which conquest takes a long, dull time. When they abandon a problem in the abrupt horse manner, they forget that this will lead to loneliness, which can consume much of their great vitality and energy.

LIFESTYLE: Horse people are perceptive and instinctive, very alert and sensitive to movements and trends. They are fond of cultural pursuits, going to theater and concerts, galleries and museums, but prefer creating their own art to appreciating that of others, and would rather make speeches than listen to them. Their idea of a good time is competition, intellectual or physical, and they are both generous winners and good losers.

FAMOUS HORSE PEOPLE: Buffalo Bill Cody, Leonard Bernstein, Josephine Baker, Georges Braque, Frédéric Chopin, Edgard Degas, Eugène Delacroix, Ulysses S. Grant, Edward Hopper, Genghis Khan, Isaac Newton, Louis Pasteur, Rembrandt,

Theodore Roosevelt, Franklin D. Roosevelt, Igor Stravinsky, the Duke of Windsor (Edward VIII).

HORSE PEOPLE BORN IN THE...

Note: Western-calendar months are given as approximations only; to find a birth moon according to the Chinese lunisolar calendar, consult the chart on pp. 30–45.

FIRST MOON (FEBRUARY): These lucky horses have a good start in childhood, leading to success in home life and at work. They are very creative and resourceful problem-solvers, friendly and open, generous and forgiving toward life. They must guard against yes-persons that can lead them to lose touch with reality and objectivity, because such people tend to gather around them.

SECOND MOON (MARCH): Stubborn and uncompromising, their character can cause trouble in collaborative work because they are very much into their own things and tend to be indulged as children, encouraged to be overly idealistic. Certainly they are reliable, honorable, and highly intelligent, but they must learn to leave space for others to grow.

THIRD MOON (APRIL): Born in the month of rising spring, these are the most active and lively horses, always galloping about. They are optimistic people who love the outdoors, and are physically healthy and clever. They favor careers involving plenty of talking, and are especially good at sales. Too many outside distractions may cause them to lose focus and patience, resulting in setbacks and depression, and they need lots of love and encouragement.

FOURTH MOON (MAY): Tremendously intelligent abstract thinkers, drawn inward by the mature yin energy of this month, they are gifted in creative fields like music and arts, philosophy, law, and the sciences. They are often absurdly comical characters, self-centered, eccentric, and apparently rather immature, but they are the true artists of the world.

FIFTH MOON (JUNE): This month of rising yang and transformation makes physically attractive horses who love to be at the center of every show and to display their luxurious tastes, glorying in material possessions. You have to admire their ability to keep up with their expenses.

SIXTH MOON (JULY): They move from place to place, looking for security and companionship, someone loving and caring who understands their dreams and ideals. They tend to marry early; if they are lucky they will find a permanent mate, but they are also likely to be disillusioned.

SEVENTH MOON (AUGUST): Opinionated and stubborn horses with the vigor to pursue their goals fearlessly. They believe their luck will never run out and their energy will last forever.They are unrealistic, perhaps, but highly creative, always on the move, never criticizing from the sidelines. They love to travel and to collect objects as well as stories from their colorful and complicated lives. Eventually they should mellow, becoming more objective and tolerant, and make very enjoyable friends.

EIGHTH MOON (SEPTEMBER): More involved in creature comforts than other horses, they love to buy things and tend to spend more than they can afford. Fortunately they are capable people, active, intelligent, helpful to friends, and perceptive of the needs of others even as they suffer their own internal struggles.

NINTH MOON (OCTOBER): The mature yin energy of this month counterbalances the mature yang energy of the Year of the Horse, so that these horses are actually more stable and solid than others. They are usually successful, applying their patience, creativity and intelligence to the arts, to business dealings, or often both. However, they have a tendency to carelessness and insensitivity in human relations that may lead them into blind behavior and emotional losses that could have been avoided.

TENTH MOON (NOVEMBER): Loners and wanderers in life, they have great potential and are willing to wait with more patience than the average horse for the right moment to come for release. They are good people who suffer much internally, and it is difficult but important for them to learn to speak up and express their need for love and care. They will have plenty of chances to meet an ideal mate and abandon their solitude and depression for parties and activities.

ELEVENTH MOON (DECEMBER): These contemplative horses are full of worries and contradictions, but their lives are full of productive surprises. Their most successful moments come at the times of greatest fear. They can be eccentric and impatient in the search for stimulating new ideas. This complex thinking can go either way: with luck, it will turn into great creative force and lead to major breakthroughs for them.

TWELFTH MOON (JANUARY OF FOLLOWING YEAR): Under the influence of the coming Year of the Ram, they have a soft and gentle side that makes them thoughtful and insightful despite their aggressive and impatient exterior, and they are likely to be successful in whatever they do.

THE LIFE CYCLE

HEALTH: Most horse people are active and outgoing, fond of outdoor activities, and therefore healthy and optimistic, with good attitudes toward life. They gallop around fearlessly, but not without danger. Most of their health traps come from within, and are problems related to stress; others are habitual indulgences that can easily be simplified or avoided with a certain amount of care. They need to pay attention to food, drink, addictive drugs, and other habits, as well as extremes of climate, which can cause them respiratory problems. Generally speaking, they are highly resilient.

MONEY: Horse people are risk takers, and can get themselves in hot financial water unless they develop a long-term strategy, patiently and without distraction. They are better off as leaders within a solid organization than investing on their own. Having said that, it should also be noted that their skill in offensive strategy, energy, and hard work make them good money makers as well as spenders. Their decisiveness and instinct make them good soldiers, usually choosing the right moment to advance or to run for shelter.

CAREER: Most horses are gifted, and their energy is unmatchable; they can fit into almost any career. Outdoor activity and mobility will be an advantage. They can be especially successful as artists and crafts persons, adventurers and explorers, designers of cars, business managers, engineers, geologists and geoscientists, lawyers, politicians, technicians and teachers, as well as in careers related to sports, communications, transportation, land, travel, and public relations

LOVE: Love is rarely of primary importance to horses, who are more focused on noble quests and glorious feats. They are physically attractive, intense and forceful, and make desirable lovers, delightful to be with, but difficult to tame. They tend to get involved in love triangles and other complicated entanglements, often bringing these imbroglios on themselves when the situation could easily have been avoided. Those who are in love with horse people must be lovers of challenge and mystery for its own sake, prepared to pay the emotional costs.

HORSE PARTNERS BORN
IN THE YEAR OF THE...

MOUSE: Opposites attract, strongly in this case, but mouse and horse are too far apart morally and emotionally for either one to make the necessary compromises, and the relationship is most likely to end in mutual rejection and betrayal. There may be some exceptions to this rule, depending on the birth moons of the people involved, but even they will not have an easy time of it.

OX: The horse is likely to suffer in this relationship, torn between attraction to the stability the ox offers and resentment at the ox's unreasonable demands. It is not likely to last long.

TIGER: These two independent characters will respect one another's needs, and their romance may become quite serious and durable. They never seem to go home, but as long as they are out partying, they are happy to be together.

RABBIT: A horse person that can learn to be patient and gentle will have a good time with the rabbit. Passion may not last, but friendship will.

DRAGON: Anything is possible with the unpredictable dragon, but this relationship is born under good auspices; the dragon and horse have many interests and ideas in common. They are also equally aggressive and there can be spectacular conflicts.

SNAKE: Neither snake nor horse is willing to make a serious commitment to the other; they are simply playing games. The one who is doing all the complaining—particularly about infidelity—is probably just as guilty as the other, and should come to a final decision as to whether it is worthwhile to continue; if it is, they will just have to try harder.

HORSE: An easy, playful relationship, perhaps a little on the superficial side, but why fight it? Two horses frisking together in the meadow are a beautiful sight, and they will have plenty of time for the serious things in life.

RAM: A romance that can end almost before it gets started, when the ram gets offended by some overly frank remark and the horse walks out. Neither one is very skilled at yielding or forgiving, and making this succeed is a little too much like work for horses to make the effort.

MONKEY: The horse is likely to be the loser in a romance with the tricky, naughty monkey, and it is not used to playing this role. If the monkey really cares, it will try to behave, make an effort to be a little more trustworthy, and things may work out.

ROOSTER: The rooster rises early, and has a lot of things on its mind, including, very possibly, a lover not born in the Year of the Horse. It may be leading the horse by the nose, as a second choice, until another lover comes through, and it will be a long time before the horse finds out—longer, perhaps, than the horse is prepared to wait.

DOG: Love at first sight and enduring friendship. The faithful, forgiving dog really understands the horse and can successfully tie it down without arousing the horse's resentment, and the horse is more dedicated to the dog than to most partners.

PIG: The pig hates to fight, but with a horse partner it just can't help it. This relationship can last for a long time, but it never gets any easier.

THE YEAR OF THE RAM

WEI

RAM YEARS

1907	February 13 to February 1, 1908
1919	February 1 to February 19, 1920
1931	February 17 to February 5, 1932
1943	February 5 to January 24, 1944
1955	January 24 to February 11, 1956
1967	February 9 to January 29, 1968
1979	January 28 to February 15, 1980
1991	February 15 to February 3, 1992
2003	February 1 to January 21, 2004
2015	February 19 to February 7, 2016
2027	February 6 to January 25, 2028
2039	January 24 to February 11, 2040

ASSOCIATIONS

EARTHLY BRANCH CHARACTER: *Wei*, meaning "not yet" and thus denoting a waiting period, the moment before something happens, and by extension moments of open possibilities and new beginnings. The essence of those born in this year is propriety. They wait with restraint for the correct time to arrive, not upsetting things when there is no need, or turning over every stone out of pure curiosity to see what lies beneath— though their analytic ability to extract every possible conclusion from information is unmatchable when there is a moral or practical aim in view.

In this they follow the precepts of Confucius, when he annoyed people in the grand temple of the dukedom of Lu by asking too many questions: "How can you say this man knows the rules of propriety," they complained, "when he asks about everything?" To which the master replied, "This is itself a rule of propriety."

ANIMAL: Three rams together with the sun symbolize the beginning of the Chinese lunar new year, and the ram *(yang)* in general represents an auspicious omen of warmth, peace, consistency, and prosperity. The Year of the Ram is regarded as an auspicious, fertile and profitable year for everybody.

As the lamb kneels before its mother in order to nurse, as if it were observing the most correct Confucian manners, so people born in the Year of the Ram are proper, patient, and moderate, with a horror of extremes. Some mistakenly regard them as weak and quiet, but in fact they are positive and constructive, applying their intelligence to the prevention of harm.

ORDER: The eighth position in the Chinese zodiac is an active and enduring position of peace. Persons born in the Year of the Ram are not fault-finders, seeking the errors of others and provoking excitement to cause trouble, but if they can point out the source of trouble in a situation or a practical way to rectify it, they will speak without fear of sounding critical.

They are good listeners, who will hear out all sides of a case to find the middle ground.

ELEMENT: Of the five Chinese elements, Earth is assigned to the Year of the Ram, in harmony with Metal, in conflict with Water, overcoming Fire but subjected to Wood. Those born in this year do well in investments and projects relating to peaceful uses of metal, minerals, and gemstones. More generally, they draw their strength from a deeply rooted sense of right and wrong; but this can also be a source of weakness in life, when their high standards make them hesitate too long to move, or give the impression that they believe themselves to be superior to others.

STAR GROUP: The Moon rules the Palace of the Year of the Ram, which houses two Lodges or Star-Spirits, Can and Jing, corresponding to stars within Orion and Gemini. Those born in the Year of the Ram are potentially in major conflict with people born in the Year of the Ox, and will need to exercise caution in dealing with them. In general they are in conflict with those who are hypersensitive to criticism, and feel attacked by the ram's calm and well-reasoned judgments. Their many friends will be those that appreciate the ram's sympathetic ear and continual delicate attentions to others' needs and pleasures.

FAVORABLE DIRECTION: South-southwest, balanced between summer and fall but more on the summery side. People born in this year will do well in projects oriented a third of the way westward from due south. Southwest is known in Chinese geomancy as one of the two "devil's doors", and it is considered dangerous to have one's bathroom, kitchen, or staircase placed in this direction, but people born in the Year of the Ram are advised to orient their front doors this way. Traveling in China, they will enjoy most the elegant foods of Hunan and the spectacular, romantic views of Guilin in Guangxi province.

FAVORABLE MONTH: Mid-August to mid-September, when hot sun alternates with showers and fresh breezes, crops ripen for the harvest, and sheep begin growing their winter coats. The full moon that rises in the evening of the fifteenth day of the Wei month is said to be the biggest and roundest of the year, and Chinese families gather in the courtyard to drink tea or strong wine, eat mooncakes (filled pastry with the round yellow yolk of a salted duck's egg at the center), and contemplate the moon's beauty, while the children run around waving colorful lanterns. Ram people enjoy waiting for things to come to fruition in the warm, placid weather, knowing that they have behaved judiciously and well deserve the coming rewards.

FAVORABLE HOUR: 1:00 PM to 3:00 PM, in the early afternoon, after a busy morning and a good lunch. This is the time when the yang power begins its decline and needs to be conserved by taking things slowly and methodically. Work in the afternoon is more peaceful and productive than the morning, with its calls and crises, and energy is gathered for new moves to ensure success for the rest of the day; wise ram people listen to their insights.

FAVORABLE NUMBERS: 3, 4, 5, 12, 34, 45, 54.

THE WHOLE PERSON

CHARACTER: People born in the Year of the Ram are gentle, patient, optimistic, intelligent, active, cautious, and fertile. They are known for their wisdom in sticking to the Golden Mean, always orderly and calm. Friendly, they are also conscious of what is owed to them, and do not hesitate to make their needs known. They are not prone to idle curiosity, but have remarkable strength and patience in searching out facts and analyzing details when there is a good reason, in matters they are called on to attend to. They do not want to use their knowledge to hurt others, even their enemies, but only to help.

Creative and imaginative, they should be given the opportunity to mull over ideas before committing to action, and to listen to all points of view. This will enable them to solve many old problems with new modifications and applications, since despite their appearance of inflexibility, they are highly adaptable in difficult situations, and excellent survivors.

EMOTIONS: Stodgy and critical as the rams seem, they are really very sensitive to others, and give a lot of energy to listening to their friends' complaints and sorrows. This is how they learn so much about moral rectitude—by taking the sufferings of others seriously. Oversensitive and self-conscious, they can be saddened by misunderstanding, and their lives often have a bittersweet character.

WEAKNESSES: Although they are usually only waiting for the right moment, rams often seem to cause unnecessary delays and frustration, and their commitment to doing things the right way gives an impression of being hypercritical and perfectionistic. At the same time, their sympathetic understanding of others leaves them vulnerable to feeling that they could be in the wrong, and they suffer a great deal from internal stress and worry. Happiness will come when they see through the ironies and contradictions of ordinary life and become more serenely confident of the rightness of their middle path.

LIFESTYLE: Ram people are fond of parties and love to plan occasions, preparing every detail in advance. On the whole, they are oriented to intellectual rather than physical pleasures, and to the traditional rather than the trendy, especially in their favorite activities, matters of high culture and gourmet eating. They can be excellent cooks, very knowledgeable about food and wine, taking great pride in their homes and kitchens, and enjoying themselves most in restaurants and food markets—they need to indulge cautiously, however, because they have delicate stomachs.

FAMOUS RAM PEOPLE: W. H. Auden, Alexander Graham Bell, Claudette Colbert, Nat King Cole, Louis Daguerre, Thomas A. Edison, Douglas Fairbanks, Thomas Gainsborough, Liberace, Franz Liszt, James Madison, Michelangelo, Laurence Olivier, Mark Twain, Rudolph Valentino.

RAM PEOPLE BORN IN THE...

Note: Western-calendar months are given as approximations only; to find a birth moon according to the Chinese lunisolar calendar, consult the chart on pp. 30–45.

FIRST MOON (FEBRUARY): Born at the peak power of the yang force, these are somewhat childlike rams, with a strong attraction to art objects, games, and hobbies that may make it hard for them to focus on serious matters. They have a great sense of individuality and openness, and are typical rams with respect to both their perfectionism and tolerance for delay.

SECOND MOON (MARCH): Hardworking and serious people who are very sensitive to criticism, they are fortunately well loved and their friends are happy to help them out in difficult times. They are intensely private and discreet, trying to avoid being upset by things, and this attitude has a certain emotional cost. They will be wise to learn the value of change, and the mix of chaos and balance in the eternal life force, *qi*.

THIRD MOON (APRIL): These extremely interesting and creative people combine the young yang force of their birth moon with the mature yang of the Year of the Ram. They are particularly brainy, excelling both at theoretical and artistic work, with unusually daring ideas. Their dangers are being too quietly critical, which may lead to isolation, and being eccentrically indifferent to their own advantage, allowing others to profit from the opportunities they have created.

FOURTH MOON (MAY): The most sociable and active of all the rams, they are physically attractive and sexy, drawing attention from others wherever they go. Gentle, neat and orderly, they enjoy all kinds of comforts, gadgets and toys. Only the best will do, of course, and the best can be quite expensive.

FIFTH MOON (JUNE): There are plenty of surprises in store, most of them are good, in the lives of these passionate, witty rams. They are sociable and talkative, friendly and smart, and their charm and resourcefulness get them attention at an early age.

They are not loners, but enjoy having a good time with other people, and their approach to life is practical and realistic.

SIXTH MOON (JULY): Those born in this month are observant and wise, poets and philosophers. Consistent and calm in everything they do, they dislike moving around, preferring to maintain strong roots and wait through storms for the better times to come. They are idealists and detail persons, but highly adaptable and practical, capable of a self-protective detachment that keeps their lives harmonious.

SEVENTH MOON (AUGUST): These gentle and honorable people are perfectionists, constantly on the lookout for the best and most beautiful things in life: luxuries, comforts, cars, clothes, cosmetics, antiques, and so on. They may regard love and power as a kind of commodity as well. Their demanding standards and ideals may be unrealistic and costly, but they always seem to be doing well and getting credit for keeping things correct.

EIGHTH MOON (SEPTEMBER): Very focused and intense, they are overly critical and skeptical. Unnecessary worry about things they cannot control makes them lose sleep at night. The fortunate side is that whatever they say attracts an audience, and they can succeed brilliantly as entertainers, including comedians and stage magicians.

NINTH MOON (OCTOBER): Rams born in this month appear especially sober and calm, but they are talented, restless and eccentric people on the inside, always with something unexpected up their sleeves. Direct and consistent in getting what they want, they are hard to resist, but they can become overly authoritarian, making things more difficult than necessary. They can divert their energy into more agreeable and friendly paths, however, and make a more productive use of their remarkable skill and intelligence.

TENTH MOON (NOVEMBER): These are unusually decisive rams, quick to act and likely to do unusual, controversial, even radical things. They seem unstable, because the quirky old yang energy of this month conflicts with the placid yang of the Ram year, making them sensitive and emotional, moody and mysterious. Their eccentricity and solitude are to some extent a theatrical pose, though, and at heart they are really quite friendly, good-hearted, helpful, and forgiving—and more successful in the long run than might be imagined.

ELEVENTH MOON (DECEMBER): Not as sociable as other rams but cordial and passive, they like to maintain a home-oriented quiet in their lives, discreetly doing their own thing. They are good people, more tolerant than most born in this year. Others may mistake their inactive position as weakness, and try to take advantage of them. They need to be cautious and sober to protect their own ground, especially in emotional matters.

TWELFTH MOON (JANUARY OF FOLLOWING YEAR): During the day, these are typical rams, calm and cautious, hard-working and keeping largely to themselves. But at night they exhibit the influence of the coming Year of the Monkey, and become lively and witty party-goers. Their office mates are amazed to see the transformation, as they become naughty and funny and apparently more talented than they were a few hours before.

THE LIFE CYCLE

HEALTH: Active and gentle, most ram people take a healthy and positive attitude toward life, but they are often delicate in health and get sick easily, being prone especially to diseases of the stomach and intestine, but also of the eye, ear, nose and throat. They need plenty of sleep and should avoid too much exposure to the sun, because their skin is sensitive. They should also be especially moderate consumers of alcohol and other addictive substances. Tending to be more intellectual than physical, they should take up exercises that are not too demanding: daily walking, gardening, dance classes, and noncompetitive swimming.

MONEY: Skillful but conservative, ram people will not take risks as the forerunners in an investment strategy, but they do their research well and know when a trend is solid and sound before others do. Thus they seem to be trend setters, especially in cultural matters, even when they are not, and they do extremely well, with enviable consistency, in money matters. They are especially tuned in to the food industry, entertainment, publishing, fashion, and the arts; on the more prosaic side they can profit from any kind of involvement with paper, metals, and minerals.

CAREER: Intelligent, patient, and quiet, those born in the Year of the Ram can fit into many different kinds of careers, as creative artists, chemists, dentists, educators, engineers, geologists, jewelers, medical professionals, programmers, scientists, technicians, politicians. They also do well in advertising, finance, management, fashion, and public relations. Where it is formally appropriate to make a lot of noise, they will not hesitate to do so, and a surprising number are great stage and screen entertainers.

LOVE: Rams are good and romantic lovers, though not impetuous or impulsive; cautious and intimate rather than hot and passionate. They rarely fall in love at first sight. They love planning a romantic picnic or evening out down to the last exquisite detail—going out with them is never a disappointment. Their affairs tend to last, because they are faithful and sensitive. It is unwise to be possessive or aggressive with a ram person, however; they will be turned off, feeling that they are being treated roughly and disrespectfully. They are much concerned with defining their territory, and hate extremes.

RAM PARTNERS BORN IN
THE YEAR OF THE...

MOUSE: Mouse and ram think they have a lot of interests and refined tastes in common, and are attracted to each other on this basis, but they misjudge each other; they are really very different deep inside, and this relationship is not easy. If it works, it is good for both sides, as the mouse becomes a little nicer and ram a little more adventurous, but it often just ends badly.

OX: Astrologically in conflict, these two are also personally incompatible, with the ox violently possessive and the ram demanding moderation. There will be terrible fights. On the other hand, as the stubbornest characters in the Chinese zodiac, neither one ever gives up, and over the very long run this couple may survive.

TIGER: The tiger yearns for the ram's unconditional respect and doesn't see why it has to take so much criticism on this minor point and that. This relationship has its pleasant moments, but is very hard to maintain, and ram will have a long wait before the tiger becomes domesticated, if it ever does.

RABBIT: The rabbit doesn't demand much more than a good time, and the ram can supply that; this is a fun romance, always out on the town. After a certain point, the ram may start sensing that there is something missing, and feel a little less happy, but they are likely to stick together through ups and downs.

DRAGON: The dragon keeps shocking the ram by changing the rules in the middle of the game; the ram starts to feel hemmed in, as if it were surrounded by four or five different dragons, and becomes uncharacteristically rebellious. Given a lot of healthy compromise, both grow in this relationship.

SNAKE: The ram brings out the worst in the snake, who is likely to be cruel, sarcastic, and deceptive. A really caring snake can learn to make an effort to be kinder, but it will take a long time for the ram to learn to trust this slippery charmer, and the romance may end long before that happens.

HORSE: Horse and ram make a funny couple, like one of those screwball comedies of the 1940s, always nipping and snapping at one another and tugging in different directions. But it may not be so amusing in the end; there is a truly negative side to all the bickering that can prevent the relationship from working out.

RAM: From the outside, this looks like an intensely dull relationship, each outdoing the other in kindness and consideration, with nothing in particular going on. If you are not a ram yourself, you will never understand what they see in one another, but you have to admit they are very happy.

MONKEY: A very bumpy romance, full of misunderstandings in the early period, but the youthful monkey yin energy and the mature ram yang complement one another nicely. If it works at all it works out very well. The most important factor is communication, and both sides are highly skilled at that.

ROOSTER: These two have the same political opinions, but they are mistaken if they think they have the same attitude toward life. The ram is continually confused by the rooster—what does it really want?—and depressed in this relationship. It is difficult, though not impossible, to make it work.

DOG: The ram tries, but doesn't appreciate the dog's loyalty; it comes on too strong, yipping at the ram's heels and trying to channel it in a direction it may not feel like going. A strong relationship, but unhappy in most cases, and the ram may eventually decide that it is time to walk out.

PIG: Pig and ram have little in common except for being exceptionally nice people. Though they are normally not attracted to each other, they may get involved more or less by accident and then stay together in order to avoid hurting each other's feelings. There's really nothing wrong with this, either, though the ram will have to do most of the work providing a sense of romance, and learn not to be resentful about it.

THE YEAR OF THE MONKEY

SHEN

MONKEY YEARS

1908	February 2 to January 21, 1909
1920	February 20 to February 7, 1921
1932	February 6 to January 25, 1933
1944	January 25 to February 12, 1945
1956	February 12 to January 30, 1957
1968	January 30 to February 16, 1969
1980	February 16 to February 4, 1981
1992	February 4 to January 22, 1993
2004	January 22 to February 8, 2005
2016	February 8 to January 27, 2017
2028	January 26 to February 12, 2029
2040	February 12 to January 31, 2041

ASSOCIATIONS

EARTHLY BRANCH CHARACTER: *Shen*, denoting the notification of one's superiors or the giving of orders to those under one's command. It is used in compounds referring to extension and expression, and hence connotes energy exploding from the center, affecting everything around it. The essence of those born in this year is irrepressibility. They are lively, physically and intellectually superb, but lacking in self-control.

ANIMAL: In Chinese folklore and art, the monkey *(hou)* represents the cunning of the mind unhindered by the heavy cares of the body and soul, most gloriously in the great Buddhist satirical novel *Xiyouji* (Journey to the West), in which the King of the Monkeys, Sun Wukong, defeats the Kings of Hell, Heaven, and the Sea, and can only be tamed by the Buddha himself, who commands him to guide the monk Tripitaka to India and bring the holy sutras back to China—a journey that gives the book its title and most of its hilarious adventures.

Monkeys are restless and active, tricky teasers, highly intelligent, highly sexed, brave and lovable animals. People born in the Year of the Monkey are strong-minded thinkers and planners, calculating and manipulative, who love to tinker with things and ideas, trying them out and changing them until they work. They work hard, but their lives are full of laughter, and though they may offend others with their jokes and tricks they are almost always forgiven.

ORDER: The ninth position in the Chinese zodiac is an active and honored one, with remarkable energy and possibilities. Wherever the monkey is, there is action, good or bad. People born in this year may seem childishly naughty, but it is not wise to think they are naive and attempt to cheat or hide things from them—they will find out and avenge themselves, turning things upside down and wreaking havoc. They are skillful leaders, but hate to admit their mistakes, blaming them on others.

ELEMENT: Of the five Chinese elements, Metal is assigned to the Year of the Monkey, in harmony with Earth and Water but in conflict with Wood and subject to Fire. People born in this year draw strength from the earth and seas, lakes and rivers, from nature and the outdoors. Their weaknesses are the distractions of civilized life, which arouse their vanity and tend to divert them from concentrating their energy in a firm and prosperous direction.

STAR GROUP: The Water Star (Mercury) rules the Palace of the Year of the Monkey, which houses four Lodges or Star-Spirits: Ang, Bi, Cui, and Jing, corresponding to stars within the Pleiades, Hyades, Taurus and Orion. Those born in this year are potentially in major conflict with people born in the Year of the Tiger. At a more everyday level, they are in conflict with everything that is ordinary, routine, and clichéd, and constantly cause quarrels with their outrageous challenges to conventional wisdom. Their support is based on their own personal wit, good humor, and attractiveness, which make even their opponents admire them.

FAVORABLE DIRECTION: West-southwest. Projects and plans directed about a third of the way south from due west are likely to succeed for those born in this year. They will be wise to design their houses with either bedrooms or living rooms facing this direction. Traveling in China, eccentric and adventurous monkeys will be most interested in following the path of the Monkey King, Sun Wukong, and heading out of China proper to the strange and beautiful mountains and monasteries of Tibet.

FAVORABLE MONTH: From mid-September to mid-October, in the beginning of fall, when the air turns crisp and the cold winter energy is invigorating, though not yet cold enough to prevent animals and insects from enjoying themselves outside. The harvest is at its most bountiful, and there are plenty of advantages waiting to be seized by energetic monkeys.

FAVORABLE HOUR: 3:00 PM to 5:00 PM, in the late afternoon, when everything seems warm and still but the hidden moon is getting ready to rise, gathering its yin energy. This is the time of day when the dark yin force is young and fierce, and concealed in the full sunlight, and monkeys are bursting to try all their tricks on the sleepy, unsuspecting yang world.

FAVORABLE NUMBERS: 3, 4, 5, 7, 16, 23, 34, 45, 54.

THE WHOLE PERSON

CHARACTER: Monkey people are clever and quick, restless, entertaining, aggressive, and sexual. They have a forceful and mercurial temperament and tend to skip steps and procedures in a task, always being able to figure out an easier way to get the job done. They are terrible teases, and sometimes worse, plotting brilliantly and taking outrageous risks to outdo their enemies. They can be disorderly and disorganized, sometimes scandalously so, and those close to them may end up cleaning up their messes, but because they are wonderfully persuasive talkers they always seem to get away with it. They tend to be physically well-formed, of average or above-average size, compactly built, and healthy.

Their fidgety, nervous character, together with their endless energy, sets them on a very different path in life from other people, and gives them a different outlook. This is a very constructive force, however, if correctly combined with an understanding of others, and many monkey people are highly successful leaders in society.

EMOTION: Monkey restlessness and outward bravery is accompanied by internal fears, both justified and unjustified, that they rarely allow people to see, and are hard for them to endure. The hot-cold, water-fire struggle causes them insecurity and misery no matter how successful they are. Vain and mischievous as they are, they are also good hearted, and truly sorry if they hurt someone unintentionally or cause embarrassing situations for their friends. At times like this they are obviously sincere, and everyone forgives them, thinking they will reform at last. They themselves are as forgiving as they expect others to be, not harboring resentment for long; they overcome hurt feelings easily.

WEAKNESSES: Their nervousness, hyperactivity, and lack of patience make monkeys apt to leap before they look, opening themselves to various dangers and traps, and threatening their chances for advancement and success. But they are so vibrant and strong, both mentally and physically, that they are quick to rebound if there is a chance to turn a situation around.

LIFESTYLE: Those born in the Year of the Monkey are full of action and energy, happiest when talking and snacking. Impatient though they may be, they are great planners and organizers of group events, taking over every party. They do not usually spend a lot of money, though with their many hobbies and activities they are not particularly good at saving it either.

FAMOUS MONKEY PEOPLE: Lord Byron, Julius Caesar, Bette Davis, Charles Dickens, Federico Fellini, Paul Gauguin, Winslow Homer, Mick Jagger, Modigliani, Grandma Moses, James Stewart, the Duchess of Windsor (Wallis Simpson), Elizabeth Taylor, Harry S Truman, Leonardo da Vinci.

MONKEY PEOPLE BORN IN THE...

Note: Western-calendar months are given as approximations only; to find a birth moon according to the Chinese lunisolar calendar, consult the chart on pp. 30–45.

FIRST MOON (FEBRUARY): Optimistic and outgoing monkeys who keep themselves busy all day long, the yang force of the zi month adding to the youthful yang of the Monkey year. Talkative, friendly and daring, they tend to be outspoken social organizers and activists who may become great leaders when issues concern them. They are great friends, charmers who hate being alone. Especially in their youth they become popular in their set as risk takers. They need to be cautious about addictions and illusory temptations.

SECOND MOON (MARCH): Fond of material things and luxuries, but also of romantic fantasies and dreams, they are obsessive in character, but their obsessions rarely last long. Often monkeys born in this month make an attempt to go into a kind of hibernation and quietly attend to their own interests, but sooner or later their friends seek them out and they quickly get involved once again; they are simply too sociable and friendly to resist.

THIRD MOON (APRIL): Aggressive and emotional, well aware of how to climb the corporate or social ladder, they will compete efficiently and ferociously with everyone, including their friends. They are protective of home and family, and less careless than other monkeys in every respect. Their aggressiveness and efficiency may be a liability as well as a strength, creating controversy and jealousy among their enemies, and they must beware of the invisible cage of isolation.

FOURTH MOON (MAY): Conflicted monkeys, torn between the youthful yang force of the Monkey Year, which wants to grab hold of everything, and the old yin of this month, which wants to let go. Moody and changeable, yet stubborn as long as the current mood lasts, smart but troublesome, they continually spring surprises on others in work and life, making things difficult for everyone. The habit of making a mountain out of every molehill will eventually diminish, but not without a price.

FIFTH MOON (JUNE): Less vain, though perhaps prouder than most monkeys, they are more easily distracted by outside influences and emotional involvement with things and people that are hard for them to reach. Excitable and nervous, they still have plenty of energy in reserve, and once it is concentrated, they are highly intelligent and capable of finding their way in life.

SIXTH MOON (JULY): These monkeys ride high and confident on the young yin energy of this month, which complements the energy of the year. Gamblers and risk takers who love to scale mountain peaks and do unusual things, they may be better at carrying out their plans than others born in this year. When they turn their world upside down, it seems to shake out better than it was before.

SEVENTH MOON (AUGUST): Creative and comparatively cautious, capable of thinking things through before they act, they seem calm and relaxed, although no one can predict what they are actually thinking or about to do. They carry naughtiness to a finely calculated art, which their friends, however annoyed, can't help admiring. Great talkers and wits, full of humor and surprises, they can be superb speech makers and may use their skills to manipulate others.

EIGHTH MOON (SEPTEMBER): Too self-conscious and concerned with details, they are insecure, constant worriers. But they have plenty of talent and capability, and are sure to succeed. If they can let things flow, they will be more relaxed and happy.

NINTH MOON (OCTOBER): Monkeys born in this month have a double dose of irrepressibility, and are the most lively, active and enthusiastic people around. Open and straightforward, they have a childlike candor and a degree of childlike absent-mindedness. They are on the earthy side, not too interested in intellectual talk and controversy, very happy outdoors. If you have to scold them, say it right out; roundabout, diplomatic expressions will annoy them and they will simply walk away.

TENTH MOON (NOVEMBER): Free spirits, but also fairly businesslike monkeys, with sharp eyes for new trends and developments, efficient and enthusiastic. They have all the monkey characteristics of energy, impatience, and restlessness, and hate to do the same old things every day, but they have more confidence than most, and this gives them a career advantage.

ELEVENTH MOON (DECEMBER): Better balanced than most of those born in the Monkey Year, less moody and restless, they are willing to compromise and share things and good at their work. Convincing communicators, friendly and humorous, they make good managers, and they are skilled coordinators of anything from choreography to housekeeping.

TWELFTH MOON (JANUARY OF FOLLOWING YEAR): Terrific story-tellers and gossips who love to exaggerate and boast, they are open and creative, outspoken and eccentric. They love travel, but may be a little tight with money and unfaithful in romance.

THE LIFE CYCLE

HEALTH: Those born in the Year of the Monkey are normally endowed with fine physical health and agility. Their biggest danger is neglect, believing that they can just keep swinging from tree to tree without suffering from their careless habits. They are weak against temptations of all kinds, and need to pay attention to what they eat, drink, sniff, and inhale. They are like children putting everything they see into their mouths, and prone to plunging into the confusion of a wrong path without giving it any forethought. Fortunately they are intelligent, aware of their problems and limitations, and will usually manage to gain the necessary self-control before it is too late.

MONEY: People born in the Year of the Monkey are skillful and brave in money matters as in others, but they need to overcome their impatience and lack of caution for issues that require long-term planning. If they do they are likely to become leaders in their field, because they really have great ability and flexibility; given their energy, they only have to develop the stability and endurance to finish the game. They are not great savers, and have to make an extra effort to plan for rainy days and retirement. Because they love nature and the outdoors, natural resources are good investment areas for them, and can help focus them on maintaining long-term goals.

CAREER: Highly intelligent and capable, creative and witty, full of energy—monkey people can fit into more or less any career they find attractive. The arts, sports, design, education, engineering, financial management, medicine, public relations, science, visual communications, and travel are good fields for them, as are careers as carpenters, geologists, land developers, and technicians.

LOVE: Monkeys are intense and active sexually, hot lovers full of passion and humor, wit and tears, laughter and quarrels. They have plenty of opportunities to meet mates at social gatherings. Given their restlessness, they are very hard to tie down, and may be downright promiscuous. A thoughtful lover gives them plenty of room and time to understand the meaning of love games. With a balance of patience and intensity they can be brought to accept the happily-ever-after end to running around.

MONKEY PARTNERS BORN IN THE YEAR OF THE...

MOUSE: The monkey will try exceptionally hard to please the mouse, without too much disciplining, because it has a lot of admiration for that sly character. In return, the mouse is flattered and charmed. These two can calm one another down and settle into domesticity almost before they realize it.

OX: The monkey has a lot to gain from the calm and patience of this companion, and in fact the ox can benefit as well. But it is up to the monkey to recognize the limits and learn how to behave, not to tease too unmercifully and not to provoke jealous rages. The ox can tolerate all the monkey's tricks as long as they do not threaten its sense of territoriality and possession.

TIGER: The tiger simply doesn't understand why other people find the monkey so attractive, and the feeling is mutual. In the rare event that these two get together, they will spend a lot of time wondering why. A very difficult relationship.

RABBIT: The rabbit may not love the monkey as much as the monkey thinks it does, but that's probably all right. The danger is when the rabbit is really serious, and then the monkey must be careful not to push too far, because it can cause a lot of unnecessary pain to this vulnerable companion.

DRAGON: This can be an ideal relationship, very romantically intense and full of enjoyment at the same time, a perfect balance of strength and intelligence. There will be difficulties, largely created just for the pleasure of working them out; they should not be taken too seriously.

SNAKE: Snake and monkey may be too sexy to resist one another initially, but sex is possibly the only thing this relationship has going for it, and it will not be enough for a lasting bond. The two find it hard to approve of each other's emotional needs and demands. If they find something else in common, they may stay together, and it could work out.

HORSE: Neither party seems to understand that this is supposed to be a love affair; they keep competing with one another. There is always a chance that they will become more mutually supportive, but they are just as likely to break up before this happens. The horse will not be flexible, and so the monkey has a big responsibility for making it work.

RAM: The monkey is crazy in love for this partner at the beginning, but will be tempted to bolt very early in the romance, when it realizes how many rules there are to be followed. Walking out will be a big mistake, however; given consideration and mutual honesty, this could be a very happy and long-lasting relationship.

MONKEY: Two monkeys together have no problems; they enjoy everything they have and don't waste time thinking about what isn't there. But separations, even brief ones, can lead to infidelity, or at the very least wounded vanity. Boring though it may be, these two should give some attention to working out ground rules.

ROOSTER: These are the opposites who attract each other beyond anybody's expectations. They disagree about almost everything, fight from the first meeting, somehow learn to tolerate each other, and then the relationship lasts forever.

DOG: Very different personalities that can complement each other. They don't seem to get along very well, and yet somehow they persist, like unwilling dance partners just trying to get through the music—then all of a sudden they are really stepping in synchrony. It takes time and practice.

PIG: For the monkey, going out with the pig feels like the purest refreshment—no hassles, no commitment, just fun in one another's company. The pig is probably madly in love, and not saying anything simply not to break the spell. The monkey should pay attention to what it is doing for once, and make that commitment.

THE YEAR OF THE ROOSTER

YOU

ROOSTER YEARS

1909	January 22 to February 9, 1910
1921	February 8 to January 27, 1922
1933	January 26 to February 13, 1934
1945	February 13 to February 1, 1946
1957	January 31 to February 17, 1958
1969	February 17 to February 5, 1970
1981	February 5 to January 24, 1982
1993	January 23 to February 9, 1994
2005	February 9 to January 28, 2006
2017	January 28 to February 15, 2018
2029	February 13 to February 2, 2030
2041	February 1 to January 21, 2042

ASSOCIATIONS

EARTHLY BRANCH CHARACTER: *You* is a picture of a clay vase or amphora in which wine is fermented; the character originally denoted spirits made from newly ripened millet. It is therefore associated with feasts and celebrations, happiness, and gratitude for success and prosperity.

The essence of those born in the Year of the Rooster is application, the ability to maintain a clear separation between activities and goals. Just as farmers put up bottles of new wine with their imaginations dwelling on future festivities, so rooster people work with great determination and skill but little love for the work itself, thinking mainly of the rewards to come. While the work is in progress, they may be both irritable and irritating, overly sensitive to criticism but harshly critical of others. They are at their most likable when the time has come to relax and celebrate their accomplishments.

ANIMAL: The rooster *(ji)* is a proud creature, the first of the diurnal animals to awaken and the one that sets the others to work with its crowing. According to one Chinese tradition, the rooster exemplifies the Five Virtues: civility, by reason of its wearing a comb; military prowess, since its legs bear spurs; courage, because it fights forward; generosity, because it calls the hens to share its food; and reliability, thanks to the regularity and precision of its crowing. But another tradition accuses the rooster of lacking in tender feelings, since it makes love looking up at the sky rather than at its mate.

Those born in the Year of the Rooster are keen, alert, and aggressive, willing to work hard to create something and to sacrifice the moment for something better in the future. They are deeply attached to tradition, but love searching out novelty as well, with good eyes and cultivated taste. They can also be temperamental and unyielding; the greater the obstacles, the greater their determination to win. They have a dangerous tendency to feel superior to others because of their ability to defer gratification. Their lives will become more balanced and their relationships more stable when they learn, sometimes late in life, that it is not necessarily good to draw so firm a line between work and play, and that greater integration leads to greater harmony with the Tao.

ORDER: The tenth position in the Chinese zodiac is one of strength, alertness, and honor. Those born in this year seek leadership positions, more out of a sense that this is appropriate for them than out of any desire for material gain. Their confidence and application help them to attain such positions. If they are careful to show respect to their subordinates, they will earn doubled respect in turn, and impressive success.

ELEMENT: Of the five Chinese elements, Metal is assigned to the Year of the Rooster, in complement with Water and Earth, but in conflict with Wood. These associations put rooster people in potentially major conflict with those born in the Wood-associated Year of the Rabbit. Given caution, knowledge, and good timing, investments related to metals and geological resources are likely to be profitable for people born in this year. More generally, roosters derive their strength from confidence that they are doing the right thing. Their chief weakness is that this confidence sometimes comes too easily, without sufficient justification. When this is the case, roosters can end up in the position they hate most—playing the part of the complacent fool. However, they have plenty of resources to help them overcome this tendency, if they can simply learn how to use them.

STAR GROUP: The Metal Star (Venus) rules the Palace of the Year of the Rooster, which houses four Lodges or Star-Spirits: Kui, Lou, Wei, and Ang, corresponding to stars within Andromeda, Pisces, Aries, Musca Borealis, and the Pleiades. The conflicts experienced by rooster people tend to stem from their own proud and unyielding nature, which may drag them into quarrels, even with their most devoted friends. They sometimes try to buy support with acts of apparent generosity, but should be warned that support gained this way will be superficial. More reliable assistance and fidelity come from those who admire the rooster's very great talents.

FAVORABLE DIRECTION: West, where the sun sets and the moon rises every evening, the home of the White Tiger, king of the beasts, whose element is Metal and who governs the autumn. The west is also home to Xi Wang Mu, the Queen Mother of the West and the guardian of the Peach Garden of Immortality, to which she invites all the gods, immortals and fairies for a banquet every ten thousand years. Those born in the Year of the Rooster should orient their projects and establishments in this direction. Traveling in China, they will have their happiest time admiring the grandeur of the Han and Tang dynasties in the ancient capitals of Luoyang and Xi'an.

FAVORABLE MONTH: Mid-October to mid-November, when the harvest is ending and Chinese peasants are at their happiest, seeing the reward of so much labor; the rooster, who calls them each morning to come out and collect the earth's bounty, feels like the host of the celebration. This is the period rooster people have been waiting for all year, when they can break the tedious routine and pause to take pride in their achievements and successes. They should not relax too much, however, and should keep their eyes open for new possibilities that may come to fruition in the following year.

FAVORABLE HOUR: 5:00 PM to 7:00 PM, the last yang hour of the day, when the setting sun shows its most glorious colors, recalling the rooster's magnificent plumage and distracting our attention from the quiet opening period of the moon. A last flurry of activity brings the day's business to an end, and workers go home to preside at the family dinner table. For the rooster, who was the first to salute the sun and has been hard at work ever since, it is time to sit back and enjoy the prestige it has earned through the day, and to rest in preparation for the next dawn.

FAVORABLE NUMBERS: 1, 5, 6, 12, 15, 16, 24, 51.

THE WHOLE PERSON

CHARACTER: Those born in the Year of the Rooster are alert and sober, conservative, powerful, decisive, and intelligent. They are brave and confident in work and life and willing to move toward new horizons. Not laid-back or easy-going, but hard-working, cautious and critical, they are well aware of their worth and tend to be proud. They are always at ease with themselves but may not get along so well with others, for their confidence may turn into conceit. Although they may be sympathetic, they are never sentimental, and rarely offer help without thinking of a *quid pro quo*.

Talented orators and conversationalists, they usually take pains over their education, which is often highly specialized, because they cannot bear to appear ignorant. They are very quick at picking up information and making use of it, becoming instant experts in many areas, which can be one of the prime factors in their success. They are also keen in the face of danger and risk.

EMOTIONS: Rooster people try to keep their emotions under control, cultivating a look of calm and even complacency that matches their self-image. However, at odd moments of distress or hurt they may erupt, which is part of the reason they can be seen as hypercritical and snappish. Quick and versatile thinkers, they sometimes speak without regard for the consequences, make enemies, and get hurt in return. Underneath, they are very emotional, longing for love and friendship that are not always easy for them to attain.

Because their sense of success depends so much on having the things they want and believe they deserve, they can be very possessive, and not always easy to like. But they are also supremely loyal and warm to those they trust, and should always be given a chance.

WEAKNESSES: The dark side of the rooster character is the sense of entitlement to credit and reward, like the rooster in the European folk tale who thought he should be congratulat-

151

ed for making the sun rise. If rooster people do not guard carefully against insensitivity to others, a tendency to selfishness may dominate. Less fortunate roosters who do not get everything they want may succumb to jealousy and envy. Loss of self-control in the grip of these emotions can lead to extremes of greed and impropriety, dishonor, and destruction that the rooster in its better moods cannot imagine. This tendency must be avoided.

LIFESTYLE: Rooster people are great givers of parties and enthusiastic guests, fond of standing around and munching on snacks and sweets as they tell anecdotes and comic stories to the admiration of a crowd. You see them at restaurants, art galleries, concerts, dance events, and hobby and craft shops. Not usually attracted to middlebrow culture, they can be slightly stuffy advocates of the most established high art, noisy adherents of the avant-garde, or sometimes both.

FAMOUS ROOSTER PEOPLE: Marian Anderson, Enrico Caruso, Catherine the Great, William Faulkner, Johann Wolfgang von Goethe, Katherine Hepburn, Rudyard Kipling, D.H. Lawrence, Groucho Marx, Cardinal Richelieu, Richard Wagner.

ROOSTER PEOPLE BORN IN THE...

Note: Western-calendar months are given as approximations only; to find a birth moon according to the Chinese lunisolar calendar, consult the chart on pp. 30–45.

FIRST MOON (FEBRUARY): Aggressive and self-centered, these roosters are also alert, perceptive, and capable of seeing both sides of an argument, which makes them especially good debaters. Their stubborn, unyielding character is balanced by more of a sense of humor than many other roosters have. Quite successful, even at an early age, they are not shy about showing off new toys to their friends.

SECOND MOON (MARCH): These roosters prefer to do things on their own and tend to reject offers of help as unnecessary.

Excellent managers and planners, they usually do not really need help anyway. Skeptical as they are about others, they are idealists on their own account, and give themselves a great deal of worry and stress by taking their work so seriously. They tend toward jealousy, and love making money and spending it on themselves.

THIRD MOON (APRIL): The youthful yang energy of this month makes them relatively relaxed and optimistic, by rooster standards. They are open and thoughtful toward others, friendly and romantic, even dreamers, but with a practical bent that makes them good at business, which is fortunate because of their love for material possessions. They are very intelligent and witty.

FOURTH MOON (MAY): These roosters tend to live in their own complex worlds, finding enough conflict within themselves without looking for more outside. They are less aggressive than others born in this year, quiet, even loners. Those who manage to get to know them find them cautious and gentle but very individualistic, indeed eccentric. They are likely to succeed as scholars or artists.

FIFTH MOON (JUNE): The explosive yang energy of this month makes them emotional and impatient, restless, and subject to hot tempers and impulsiveness. They are open to extremes of good and bad; their potential is great but they must make the choice of their destiny. With discipline and training they can become great creative forces, breaking through to new ideas.

SIXTH MOON (JULY): These are creative roosters, idealistic people who will work relentlessly to achieve their dreams. They are impatient perfectionists, and this makes them moody and rather unpredictable, difficult to understand. Their inner conflicts often frustrate those close to them. Though they seem indecisive and troublesome, they are very honorable people.

SEVENTH MOON (AUGUST): Less self-centered and also less extroverted than other roosters, they are free and generous persons with attractively childlike qualities, but should not be regarded as weak. They are highly creative, and quick decision-makers, which could get them into trouble, as their plans may contradict one another. At the same time, they are cautious and slow to act, so that after long periods of apparent indecision, they always seem to have made their move with perfect timing.

EIGHTH MOON (SEPTEMBER): These appear more modest than other roosters, sociable and unassuming, always asking questions instead of telling you about themselves, but they are very creative and endowed with a will of their own. They rarely follow instructions or take a conventional path to any goal, instead coming up with new and seemingly convoluted methods to achieve what they want—often with results as good as or better than those delivered by a more normal approach.

NINTH MOON (OCTOBER): Raging internal conflicts make them subject to terrible worries and anxieties as well as powerful ambitions and desires. They tend to keep these bottled up, making supreme efforts to stay calm on the outside until the time for action arrives. They may be deeply unhappy but are also extraordinarily gifted, capable of turning their explosive character into stunning creative success.

TENTH MOON (NOVEMBER): The feast starts early for these cheery roosters. They are like well-behaved but slightly greedy children, easily talked into all kinds of escapades and always running out to buy a new toy. They grow more sophisticated, but not less acquisitive, and those toys can end up getting quite expensive. The double dose of rooster wit is always entertaining, as long as it is not aimed at you, and they are lots of fun to be with.

ELEVENTH MOON (DECEMBER): A good balance of yin and yang forces gives them equal parts of talent and luck, getting them attention wherever they go, even at a very young age. Generous and optimistic, they are especially gifted in anything to do with speech and language, and may be great entertainers, particularly storytellers and actors.

TWELFTH MOON (JANUARY OF FOLLOWING YEAR): These are the most sentimental roosters, perceptive and intelligent, reserved and serious. They tend to be especially sensitive about cleanliness and personal appearance, and like to dress in a showy, artistic, but not offensive way. They are pleasant and orderly in manner, graceful, with good-humored wit.

THE LIFE CYCLE

HEALTH: Roosters are usually active and healthy, but they suffer from a certain restlessness and anxiety stemming from a continual emotional struggle for balance. Fond of going out, they face constant temptations to overindulge in substances, sex, and emotions. Excessive lifestyle habits make them vulnerable to intestinal and respiratory troubles. They are also sensitive to extremes of hot and cold climate, and are most happy and active in subtropical and temperate zones.

MONEY: Those born in the Year of the Rooster are alert and keen at spotting profitable deals, especially those involving new trends and fashions,and anything involving the rooster element of Metal. They also know how to promote their efforts strategically to maximize profit. Many roosters are top leaders in the financial world, using their creativity and competence to examine every possible way of winning the game.

CAREER: With their talent and alertness, most rooster people have a wide range of careers that will suit them. They may be artists, architects, designers, educators, engineers, entertainers, financial managers, geologists, gem experts, politicians, or technicians, or succeed in fields such as land and mineral development, music, medicine, the military, visual communications, and public relations.

LOVE: The emotional and possessive character of the rooster extends to matters of love and sex. They may regard sexual attraction as a game, but they play it intensely and creatively. They may be unfaithful, but not disloyal—at least not as they regard disloyalty. They are the type of person who can maintain more than one serious relationship, such as a marriage and an affair, without feeling guilty, because they are perfectly attentive to both. Because of their restless anxiety and impatience they tend to be attracted more to those who are secure, patient, and caring. They prefer to be the only critic in a relationship. Their love quarrels are noisy and may become notorious. Highly sexed, they are also highly fertile, and likely to have an above-average number of children.

ROOSTER PARTNERS BORN IN THE YEAR OF THE...

MOUSE: These two can be good, competitive buddies, but a romance is not likely to last, since mouse finds it very hard to trust rooster's sincerity. If the rooster is serious, it had better prepare for hard times, because this will be a combative relationship. Even an unhappy mouse can't resist poking fun, and knows all the rooster's weakest points.

OX: Ox has a very good time with rooster, uncharacteristically enjoying going out on the town, and gives a great deal in return. Both are very stubborn, and there will be fights, but the rooster should be patient, because these are not quarrels over territory, and will probably have a happy ending.

TIGER: These two have very different values, and although they may be strongly attracted to one another it is difficult for them to communicate. Each holds its ground, and mutual friends, constantly called in to serve as peacemakers, may eventually get tired of doing the communication for them.

RABBIT: The rooster may be attracted to the gentle, passive rabbit, envisioning a perfect relationship from the rooster point of view. It is in for a surprise, because a relationship with a rooster creates a new, angry rabbit, spoiling for a fight. You can't make a rope by twisting metal into wood, and the chances for this working out are very poor.

DRAGON: This is the relationship of rooster's dreams, the one that makes it vulnerable and liberates it from the demands of the ego—true love. But after awhile the rooster begins to wonder if this wonderful person is for real. Only time will tell if the dragon is willing to come down from the clouds and agree to live on solid common ground. It can happen, though, and if it does, the rooster will be very happy.

SNAKE: The rooster wakes up early, ready to go, and the snake complains—it wants to go back to sleep. These two bicker quite a bit, though it is not in snake's nature to be argumentative. It hardly seems as if anything worthwhile is going to happen, but things are going on in that deep snake mind, and if rooster applies some patience, a lasting relationship may result.

HORSE: The horse is probably not interested enough to make the requisite effort. It likes going out with the rooster and showing it off to its friends, but will not make a commitment. When things get bad, neither side is willing to take the blame. The rooster will have to be uncharacteristically humble to make this work.

RAM: Both partners are interested in following the rules, but are not necessarily playing the same game, and it may take a long time for them to find this out. In the patience stakes, the ram beats the rooster every time, but the rooster's impatience is likely to be bad for both parties.

MONKEY: In the short run the problems seem insuperable. But there's something about the monkey that the rooster hates to abandon, and it will keep trying. The monkey is just wicked enough to defend itself, and the rooster admires that. A happy relationship, once initial difficulties are overcome.

ROOSTER: Feathers fly, and blood may be drawn as well, but two roosters have so much in common with each other (and with no one else) that they may stick together in self-defense. It's not such a bad thing, either, though they will be happier if they learn that kissing is easier than fighting.

DOG: These two fussy characters enjoy chatting about this and that, but they are not likely to become intimate with each other. If they do, the rooster may find the bark better than the bite, and get out in a hurry. This is not an easy relationship, and it may be advisable not to try too hard.

PIG: The lovable pig gives the rooster everything it longs for: respect, admiration, and a lot of fun as well. The rooster may be thinking it could gain more status with another lover, but it is mistaken. The pig isn't stupid, merely nice, and has a good deal of the kind of wisdom that rooster lacks. If the rooster is smart, it will learn how to learn from such a companion, and become a little more pig-like itself.

THE YEAR
OF THE
DOG

XU

DOG YEARS

1910	February 10 to January 29, 1911
1922	January 28 to February 15, 1923
1934	February 14 to February 3, 1935
1946	February 2 to January 21, 1947
1958	February 18 to February 7, 1959
1970	February 6 to January 26, 1971
1982	January 25 to February 12, 1983
1994	February 10 to January 30, 1995
2006	January 29 to February 17, 2007
2018	February 16 to February 4, 2019
2030	February 3 to January 22, 2031
2042	January 22 to February 9, 2043

ASSOCIATIONS

EARTHLY BRANCH CHARACTER: *Xu* is a picture of a halberd—a type of battle-ax mounted on a pole—with the wound it causes represented by the horizontal stroke on the left. It denotes the action of attacking, but its connotations are positive ones, relating to timeliness in action, usefulness, and involvement; and by extension to strength and energy of intent. The essence of those born in the Year of the Dog is watchfulness. They are always the first to warn against approaching danger, and mix alert and quiet caution with great boldness when the time is right to act. Their restlessness grows after sundown, when the yin force comes into its own.

ANIMAL: The dog *(gou)* is famous in China, as elsewhere in the world, for its love and loyalty toward its friends and its ferocity toward the enemies of its friends. It has few enemies of its own, and people say that since everyone loves a dog, those born in this year will always be loved by their spouses. Another folk belief is that dog people born in the night hours are doomed to suffer and struggle, like watchdogs who must remain alert while the family members snore in their beds, while those born in the daytime will be more comfortable in life.

Those born in the Year of the Dog are intelligent, faithful, sociable, and strong. They have excellent instincts and perceptions, and work hard to carry out their responsibilities at work and in their personal lives. They are usually well-mannered and graceful in appearance, and these advantages often bring them advancement, which they repay with their trustworthiness and skill. Once successful, they rarely lose out.

ORDER: The eleventh position in the Chinese zodiac is powerful and active. Although people born in the Year of the Dog often seem quiet, they are always internally restless and frequently talk behind others' backs, readying the ground for action. When ready to act they proceed fearlessly and methodically to resolve all the obstacles that lie ahead, which makes many of them very successful leaders, well prepared and rarely asking a subordinate to do something they cannot do themselves.

ELEMENT: Of the five Chinese Elements, Earth is assigned to the Year of the Dog, giving birth to Metal, but in conflict with Fire and Water. People born in this year draw strength from the earth and the metal deposits that lie within it, and tend to succeed in investments and careers related to land, minerals, and metals. Their strength is innate, and their weakness, perhaps, a tendency to rely too much on this inner strength instead of looking for help and comfort from others.

STAR GROUP: The Fire Star (Mars) rules the Palace of the Year of the Dog, which houses three Lodges or Star-Spirits: Shi, Bi, and Kui, corresponding to stars within Pegasus, Andromeda, and Pisces. People born in this year are potentially in major conflict with those born in the Year of the Dragon. In a more general sense, they are in conflict with everything they regard as showy, insincere, and disloyal. They are protectors of the humble and unpretentious, and these small folk will always be ready to support them in time of need.

FAVORABLE DIRECTION: West by northwest; projects, ideas, and plans oriented a third of the way north from due west will be beneficial to those born in this year. They might want to think especially about orienting their work desks or bedroom doors in this direction. Traveling in China, their love of rugged terrain and interest in military matters might lead them to enjoy a side trip on the route of the Long March to Yan'an. They should not miss the chance to visit the splendid grasslands of Inner Mongolia, drink butter tea, and spend the night in a yurt.

FAVORABLE MONTH: Mid-November to mid-December, the beginning of winter, when animals, insects, and plants enter a state of quiescence. The dog, alone of all the domestic animals, remains alert, guarding the home against intruders, ready to frighten them away with its bark or attack them if necessary. Dog people should enjoy all the celebrations and parties of this period, when the harvest is finished and work in the fields has come to an end. But they should also remain watchful for opportunities that present themselves when others are not looking, and for the dangers that arise in silence.

FAVORABLE HOUR: 7:00 PM to 9:00 PM, when the dark yin power first establishes itself for the night. It is a warm and happy moment, as the family lights the candles and gathers for dinner, taking care that the household dogs feel loved, well fed, and trusted as nighttime protectors. It is also the the beginning of the nightly vigil for those born in the Year of the Dog, who are night creatures to the core, restless and wary, but also ready for a good time.

FAVORABLE NUMBERS: 1, 4, 5, 10, 14, 19, 28, 30, 41, 45, 54.

THE WHOLE PERSON

CHARACTER: People born in the Year of the Dog make good friends. They are attractive, witty, magnetic personalities, with an optimistic nature that sees life as full of opportunity and excitement—excitement that does usually come to them. Quick but cautious, moving only when they feel confident, they tend to be defensive players. Though they are fighters, they are also survivors who know the right moment for a retreat. Restless and active, they are bored if things drag on too long or become too easy, but they are never afraid of hard work.

Success may be a long time in coming, despite their loyalty and skill, and some dog people seem doomed to slog away in unrecognized toil, but eventually their plans will pay off. In the meantime, they get a lot of consolation from their outside interests—physical activities, hobbies, and socializing.

EMOTIONS: Loyalty to others is the key element in the dog's emotional makeup, whether to colleagues, friends, or lovers. They are highly sensitive to the possibility that others may not be as deeply attached as they are. Since their feelings are easily hurt, and their memories long, emotional damage will take time to heal, but eventually they will return to their original happy enthusiasm. In spite of their careful planning and their patience in waiting for the opportune moment, powerful dog emotions may lead them into dangerously impulsive behavior, and this must be guarded against.

WEAKNESSES: Unbridled optimism may lead dog people into disappointment and disillusion. Overconfidence can get them involved in more things than they can handle. Belief in their own good intentions may also make them feel that barriers are bound to melt away, and when this does not happen they will feel cheated. They need to learn to examine themselves as closely as they examine others, because their intentions may not be as good as they assume. Resourcefulness and resilience help them to overcome most temporary difficulties, however terrible they may seem at a particular moment.

LIFESTYLE: Night people, those born in the Year of the Dog get wound up at the start of the *xu* hour (from 7:00 PM) and love to keep going till dawn, talking, dancing, and doing what comes naturally. They work hard and seriously during the day, and certainly deserve all the relaxation, entertainment, and good food they crave, but they should be careful not to overindulge and overspend. With their positive attitude and adaptability, they love travel, and benefit when they are on the road from a keen sense of direction and a sensitivity to foreign environments. Work is always a priority, but they love to keep active when they are not working, especially in arts and in competitive sports, or any kind of outdoor or nature-oriented activity.

FAMOUS DOG PEOPLE: Winston Churchill, Alexander Calder, Benjamin Disraeli, Benjamin Franklin, Robert Frost, Judy Garland, Victor Hugo, Michael Jackson, Vladimir Lenin, Henry Moore, Socrates, Gertrude Stein, Voltaire, Zhou Enlai.

DOG PEOPLE BORN IN THE...

Note: Western-calendar months are given as approximations only; to find a birth moon according to the Chinese lunisolar calendar, consult the chart on pp. 30-45.

FIRST MOON (FEBRUARY): Spiritual and non-materialistic, they can be somewhat careless about money. They would rather enjoy themselves than merely accumulate, and should take care to keep an umbrella ready for a rainy day. Very witty, but also very trustworthy, they make good friends. Their early life can be uneven, but they will weather the storm and reach a safe harbor.

SECOND MOON (MARCH): Equally powerful mature and youthful yin forces pull these moody and changeable dogs in opposite directions, especially in matters of love, where they may be less loyal than in other kinds of relationships. They are sexy and passionate, and many people love them for their wit, energy, and fun. At work they are serious and conscientious, bringing plenty of imagination and often artistic talent to the job.

THIRD MOON (APRIL): Great communicators and lucky people, gifted with ambition and creativity, they make superb salespeople and politicians. They will stubbornly hold on to a point of view or tactic at practically any cost, and rarely admit when they have been wrong or unfair. They need to take care not to overdo things, as their luck will not always hold.

FOURTH MOON (MAY): These cheery dogs gain lots of mileage with their big smiles, making others feel comfortable. They can use this to manipulate their way to success, not so much out of dishonesty, but as an obvious tactic. They are great and intelligent game players, and usually get what they want.

FIFTH MOON (JUNE): Often conceited, they may be snobbish toward their friends, which can be costly, as can their love for social gatherings and beautiful things. But they have good reasons for confidence, as their analytic ability gives them an early edge against competitors in many areas.

SIXTH MOON (JULY): Intellectual dogs, with flexible minds and great verbal skills, they are also good organizers and resolute workers. They are likely to accumulate a wide variety of experience in life, and to succeed in a number of different paths.

SEVENTH MOON (AUGUST): Fierce inner conflicts paralyze them at times; they are certainly the least physically active of dog people, and among the most intellectual, analyzing everything they come across. They shine as detectives, critics, researchers and professionals. Despite their achievements, their confidence can be wounded by a feeling that they have not gone far enough, and by skepticism as to whether their work will pay off, and this may stand in the way of further advancement.

EIGHTH MOON (SEPTEMBER): These dogs are perfectionists, dissatisfied with themselves and everything else. Because they procrastinate and scatter their attention from one dissatisfaction to another, they appear careless and disorganized, moody and changeable. They need to discipline themselves to stick to a plan and show up on time, and also guard against certain addictions and habits. Free spirits in their social relations and always abreast of fashion, they are fun to be with, but can be annoying when things get serious.

NINTH MOON (OCTOBER): A surplus of young yin energy makes them active, perceptive, and cunning from an early age, and they will attract plenty of attention, though they may be loners. They are orderly, patient, and reliable, but like to work creatively behind the scenes and at their own pace, and they are always in danger of becoming isolated and infected with unrealistic ideas. Their friends appreciate their generosity but may hesitate to be frank with them.

TENTH MOON (NOVEMBER): No detail escapes the eyes of these alert dogs, and they are highly gifted at any kind of observation and research. They are brave as well, especially in attacking falsehood and deception, because truth is very important to them. Hardworking and serious, they may suffer from sensitivity and self-consciousness, due to the workings of their overactive minds.

ELEVENTH MOON (DECEMBER): These warm, passionate people attract friends wherever they go with their thoughtful consideration and generosity. They need a lot of support as well, because they are worriers who spend sleepless nights turning plans and problems over and over in their heads, to the point of undermining their self-confidence.

TWELFTH MOON (JANUARY OF FOLLOWING YEAR): Torn between duty and frivolity, they will work themselves to the bone to save money and then blow it all on a single spending spree. Basically, however, stability is their top priority, and they are highly home-oriented, not terribly interested in dazzling others.

THE LIFE CYCLE

HEALTH: Dog people are usually quite healthy and fit, keeping themselves in shape with plenty of exercise, and benefiting from an enthusiastic attitude that keeps them going even in the darkest moments. They do need to pay attention to daily health, however, and even the most skillful need to watch out for problems caused by overeating, too much alcohol, fast driving, and risky adventures. Eventually they will almost always learn moderation, but early is better than late.

MONEY: Those born in the Year of the Dog are great defenders of their own homes and security, but are also aggressive. They may be reckless spenders when it comes to personal pleasure, but are most likely to be conservative overall, guarding their money carefully with a superb nose for risk that makes them very skillful in management and investment. Especially suitable areas of investment include anything to do with land, food, travel, or metals, including construction and manufacturing. They can manage several projects at the same time without losing track, although they need to be careful about carrying this too far; overconfidence can land them in tight spots that no amount of skill can get them out of.

CAREER: Hard workers and highly intelligent, dog people can make fine careers in many different fields, including land development, food-related industries, mineral and metal-related business, public relations, the military, politics, and anything related to sports. They are also talented as artists, architects, educators, engineers, geologists, jewelers, researchers, scientists, and technicians.

LOVE: Emotional attachment is never a casual matter to those born in this year. A sense of love and belonging is critical to their well-being, and they are possessive, defensive, and patient with difficult partners, apparently blind to their defects. They may be attracted to many, but they cannot bear breaking off relationships, and will stick with a bad one until it becomes intolerable. Most partners appreciate their kindness, though some will be irritated by their anxious concern.

DOG PARTNERS BORN IN
THE YEAR OF THE...

MOUSE: Too many nerves are involved in this relationship for one not to get on the other's. Mouse and dog may make each other uncomfortable much of the time, and the mouse may be pretending to cooperate while secretly plotting to escape. It is up to the dog not to push too hard, giving the mouse space and time, if this very difficult relationship is to last.

OX: It is hard for the dog to make a commitment to this relentless partner, and it may be wise for it to hold back, because both the ox and the dog insist on playing the same role, the stable and generous protector. Neither is willing to sit back and simply be protected and happy, so that even with the best intentions this relationship can quickly degenerate into a grim power struggle.

TIGER: The dog and tiger fight when they don't know each other well, in part to conceal a deep attraction for one another. When they recognize this for what it is, they are likely to find a very good relationship, full of mutual respect, good times, and passion.

RABBIT: The dog is aware of very few tensions with the rabbit. Each seems to bring to the relationship what the other lacks, so that together they are like one perfect person. Even if romantic sparks do not fly, which can happen when there is so little friction, the dog has made a good friend and will have nothing to regret.

DRAGON: The dog is fascinated and tempted by the dragon, but there are many reasons for staying away from this lover besides the astrological belief that they are incompatible. Either the dragon is playing games, about to transform itself into a creature of the air and fly into the clouds, leaving the dog earthbound, bruised, and possibly bleeding; or else the dog's own intentions are less than honorable and it ends up doing something impulsive and possibly tragic.

SNAKE: Snake and dog do not communicate well, and are not likely to attract one another in the first place. They underestimate each other's intelligence, having very different habits. If they should get involved, the dog must have plenty of patience and be prepared for a certain amount of grief, since snake people have difficulty with sexual fidelity. But both are honorable at heart, and things may work out.

HORSE: The horse has little patience for the dog's style of love, and will make an effort not to get caught, but a determined dog can succeed. Once the horse is caught, things will change in a radical way: the expected outcome of this romance is quite positive.

RAM: Dog and ram very often get together on the basis of mutual attraction, and then wonder why. They don't seem to agree about anything, quarrel constantly, and neither has the courage to put an end to the affair. It rarely does end, for better or for worse, and worse is frequently what it is, in the form of an unhappy marriage. The dog, with its instinctive courtesy, could try to make it better.

MONKEY: The monkey is naive and goodhearted in many areas of life, but can be manipulative and wickedly selfish in matters of sex. If the dog wants to avoid being badly hurt, it should be very cautious, not judge on the basis of first impressions, and try to keep an emotional distance.

ROOSTER: Like many others, the dog finds its temper sorely tried by this vain and sometimes ridiculous bird, but they have a good time together, especially at first. Eventually, if it lasts, the dog will realize how vulnerable the rooster actually is and feel quite noble protecting it. But things will still be difficult.

DOG: Two dogs can be great friends, though quarreling incessantly and competing intensely. This kind of competition does not work in romance. Even when they try to compromise, each will try to outdo the other in sacrifices, and they will be no better off than before. It takes a great deal of delicacy on both sides to make this work.

PIG: Early on, the pig senses the dog's nervousness, and is somewhat unsure how to interpret it; the dog should resolutely ignore any little difficulties of this kind. The pig is only pinching itself to make sure it is not dreaming. This is a very happy and romantic relationship that will never end.

THE YEAR OF THE PIG

HAI

PIG YEARS

1911	January 30 to February 17, 1912
1923	February 16 to February 4, 1924
1935	February 4 to January 23, 1936
1947	January 22 to February 9, 1948
1959	February 8 to January 27, 1960
1971	January 27 to February 14, 1972
1983	February 13 to February 1, 1984
1995	January 31 to February 18, 1996
2007	February 18 to February 6, 2008
2012	January 23 to February 9, 2013
2024	February 10 to January 28, 2025
2036	January 28 to February 14, 2037
2048	February 14 to February 1, 2049

ASSOCIATIONS

EARTHLY BRANCH CHARACTER: *Hai* is originally related to the character for *shi*, an old word for pig, but it has also been interpreted as representing a man and woman making love beneath the sky, thus referring to the begetting of children with the cooperation of Heaven; it denotes the auspicious moment when a new cycle begins out of the old one, and by extension the presence of beginnings within endings of all kinds.

The essence of those born in this year is resignation, accepting the world as it is, with the understanding that all things are cyclical and their nature cannot be changed. They are more likely to be wise but passive observers than actors in important events. Though warm and generous in private relationships—and even capable of great stubbornness where their emotions are engaged—they are shy and modest in public. They are keenly aware of human absurdities, and this gives them an advantage in survival over the long haul..

ANIMAL: The pig *(zhu)* is an easily contented animal, living humbly from day to day for the pleasure the day provides. Many Chinese hold it in low esteem, as do many other cultures, though only the strictest vegetarians go so far as to abjure eating its flesh, as Jews and Muslims do. In the novel *Xiyou Ji* (Journey to the West) the Pig Spirit Zhu Bajie represents pure sensual appetite without self-control; but he is also a well-loved character, because he openly and good-naturedly admits to feelings we all harbor. In traditional rural China, pigs were as much a part of the family as dogs, wandering freely inside the house and helping to pick up food from the floor. Indeed, the character *jia* ("home"or " family") is a picture of a pig under a roof, as if to say a good home is one where pigs are kept.

Farmers who raise pigs will tell you that they are among the most intelligent of domestic animals, curious and knowledgeable and good at making complicated plans. Those born in the Year of the Pig are also highly intelligent, but unwilling to apply their intelligence to dominating others and achieving high position. Whether concerned with dinner or with abstruse scholarly matters, they work for pleasure rather than the

171

advantages they might obtain, and this may lead others to undervalue them.

ORDER: The twelfth and last position in the Chinese zodiac is a very powerful one, as the last and final linkage to the beginning of a coming cycle. Underappreciated in their early lives because of their unwillingness to push themselves forward, eventually those born in this year can hope to be recognized for their wisdom and kindness, and may find themselves in high positions. Those who are skilled and dedicated will be lucky to work under them, for they have a special gift for reintegrating what has become fragmented, and govern according to the Taoist principle, seeking harmony above all, and never interfering with what is going well.

ELEMENT: Of the five Chinese elements, Water is assigned to the Year of the Pig, giving life to Wood but in conflict with Fire, and subject to Earth. Water is a symbol of prosperity in Chinese tradition, nourishing and refreshing all creation. People born in this year draw strength from nature, giving life to everything; their weaknesses come from a tendency to let things evolve in due course, without attempting to play an active role in the process.

STAR GROUP: The Wood Star (Jupiter) rules the Palace of the Year of the Pig, which houses three Lodges or Star-Spirits: Xu, Wei, and Shi, corresponding to stars within Aquarius, Equuleus, and Pegasus. Those born in this year are potentially in major conflict with those born in the Year of the Snake. Normally, they have few conflicts in life, being unwilling to stick their necks out, or perhaps too wise to fight except on behalf of others who appreciate and love them. Given such support, however, they gain confidence and become firmer in the adoption of goals, and will eventually fight as relentlessly as wild boars if it seems necessary.

FAVORABLE DIRECTION: North by northwest; people born in this year will increase their good fortune by orienting their plans and projects a third of the way west from due north . Traveling in China, they should not neglect the ancient Shang Dynasty archaeological sites at Anyang, a powerful reminder of the cyclical nature of all things, and should cool down and relax amid the beautiful hills and temples of Taiyuan.

FAVORABLE MONTH: Mid-December to mid-January, at the end of the lunisolar year, when everyone is busily preparing for the feasts and celebrations of the New Year holiday. Animals, birds and insects are quiescent, but humans are at their most active, and the pig, the most humanlike of all the domestic animals in its love for peace and fun, is in a festive mood as well. On the last evening of the month families will gather for a formal reunion dinner to reinforce their solidarity and love for one another, and this is a time when those born in the Year of the Pig should pause to take stock of what they have accomplished in the old year and exchange ideas on what they can do in the new.

FAVORABLE HOUR: 9 PM to 11 PM, when the yin force grows in strength and stability and people get ready for bed, thankful to be home again, fed and sheltered for the night, healthy and alive. As the cycle of the day draws to a close, it is wise to reevaluate one's actions in terms of what they mean to one's own life and their possible effects on others, listening to the quiet voice, clearer in the dark, of the inner self.

FAVORABLE NUMBERS: 1, 3, 4, 8, 16, 18, 34, 41, 48.

THE WHOLE PERSON

CHARACTER: Those born in the Year of the Pig are peaceful but alert, optimistic but passive, intelligent but shy, generous but afraid of ridicule, and often highly artistic. They have a strong sense that the world is dangerous and full of traps, and they prefer to stay out of public attention and behind the front lines. They rarely find an issue over which they are willing to be stubborn, but when they do, they can be fiercely combative and unwilling to accept defeat. Sensitive and gentle, generous to their friends but not personally extravagant, they are very serious about sensual pleasures, including the arts. They are fond of exploring nature, but happiest at home. Shy though they may be, social life is very important to them, and they love the kind of parties where food and gossip are the main items.

EMOTIONS: Pig people are warm and attached to others, feeling deeply, despite a tendency toward reserve, especially in public. They are disinclined to openly communicate their emotions. They take a sensual delight in everything, even intellectual or philosophical matters that seem quite abstract to other people. They can be melancholy when things do not go right, or when they feel that they have not carried out their own responsibilities properly. They make wonderful, undemanding friends and have few enemies; their emotional wounds heal well and they are very forgiving.

WEAKNESSES: Despite their wisdom in understanding the cyclical nature of things and their joy in the sensual, pigs—especially those involved in creative work—can be subject to gloom and depression. They are perfectionists, especially with regard to their personal responsibilities, and not achieving what they envision causes them serious internal stress. They tend to keep these sorrows bottled up inside, rarely opening up to friends during their periodic crises, and can wind up stuck in isolation and self-absorption. They may see their unhappiness as a necessary experience in the development of their creative powers, but must beware of carrying it too far into conflict and disillusion.

LIFESTYLE: Domestically inclined, those born in this year are especially fond of keeping their homes well appointed, comfortable, and elegant. They like travel, but only within strict limits, shopping enthusiastically for exotic food and clothes, but soon finding themselves longing for home. In fashion, they are imaginative and artistic, presenting themselves beautifully, but they are also conservative, and prefer to wait for others to try out the trends before adopting them themselves. They take food and entertainment very seriously, as well as culture and the arts, finding a physical pleasure even in the most intellectual matters. Their interest in hobbies can be intense, sometimes leading them to become full-time collectors or professionals in areas that had once been mere diversion.

FAMOUS PIG PEOPLE: John Quincy Adams, Otto von Bismarck, Maria Callas, Paul Cézanne, Marc Chagall, Henry Ford, Ernest Hemingway, Thomas Jefferson, Carl Gustav Jung, Kublai Khan, Thomas Mann, Georgia O'Keeffe, Tennessee Williams, Johnny Mathis.

PIG PEOPLE BORN IN THE...

Note: Western-calendar months are given as approximations only; to find a birth moon according to the Chinese lunisolar calendar, consult the chart on pp. 30–45.

FIRST MOON (FEBRUARY): These pigs are quiet and somewhat self-conscious, yet they are also very persuasive when they start talking, and will have much success in sales careers and in love affairs—sometimes more success than they can handle. Good fortune tends to follow them, and their lives are eventful and full of opportunities.

SECOND MOON (MARCH): Very concentrated pigs, who can lose their detachment once they get involved with a thing or person. Obsession can put obstacles in their way to success, but they are confident and intelligent, and armed with good intentions. Good luck usually keeps them out of harm's way.

THIRD MOON (APRIL): Their minds are full of marvelous ideas and projects they feel unable to carry through. This is unfortunate, because they are much more capable than they think. To some extent they may be making excuses; if something is preventing them from making a breakthrough, it may be less a matter of self-confidence than a lack of necessary endurance. If they understand this, they can learn to be more patient.

FOURTH MOON (MAY): More physically robust than most pig people, they are active and even athletic, with an easy-going approach to life. Joking and showing off their toys are enough to keep them happy, at least until mid-life. At that point a turbulent crisis is likely to occur, and its final outcome may be uncertain.

FIFTH MOON (JUNE): These are among the most creative and artistic pigs, very involved with private games and secret objects. Sentimental and passionate in human relations, they are reserved and skeptical about ideas other than their own, with which they may become obsessed, either dangerously or productively. Fortunately, they can be quite efficient at channeling their energy toward success.

SIXTH MOON (JULY): They may take the pig's passivity a bit too far, cultivating an air of mystery and mulling over ideas while others do the work. Once they finally make up their minds to pursue something they show unexpected skill and efficiency, surprising everyone. Warm and attractive, they have plenty of friends, but love to keep people guessing, acquiring a reputation for being difficult to understand.

SEVENTH MOON (AUGUST): These highly energetic, active pigs make plenty of noise, but they work as hard as quieter people, conquering obstacles one at a time. Talkative and witty, they are better able to overcome their shyness than other pigs, willing to challenge their opponents' views and ideas. This, combined with their creativity, makes them good entertainers, actors, or comedians.

EIGHTH MOON (SEPTEMBER): Tension between youthful yin and ripe yang energy makes them nervous and somewhat oversensitive. Perfectionists, they are good planners, especially for group events and activities, but they like to do all the work and worrying by themselves and tend to overdo both. However, they secretly enjoy their constant anxiety, which keeps them busy, and in any case are very good at whatever they do.

NINTH MOON (OCTOBER): Highly intellectual, analytical, and self-critical, they exist in a constant state of insecurity and mental turbulence that leads them to regard everything—from a trip to the bank to weeding the vegetable garden—as a philosophical problem. They often appear comically absent-minded, matching the wrong color scarf and getting off the train at the wrong stop. But they are open, passionate, reliable, friendly, hard-working, and creative, and should have plenty of good luck in life.

TENTH MOON (NOVEMBER): Old yang energy makes them the most conservative of pigs, dependent on stable and consistent environments and disturbed by movement and change around them. At the same time, they are relatively brave and outspoken people, which can lead them to offend others without realizing it. Friends should not forget that under their prickly exterior they are as goodhearted, trusting, and concerned as others born in this year.

ELEVENTH MOON (DECEMBER): These pigs are very friendly but somewhat difficult to live with, defensive in personal matters and with a desire for control. They work hard and efficiently, taking an analytical approach to problems. They are optimistic and decisive, practical, and dedicated to their careers, making heavy demands on themselves and others.

TWELFTH MOON (JANUARY OF FOLLOWING YEAR): Quiet and generous, very intelligent but capable of great foolishness, they are always in danger of being dominated by their friends. Outwardly they seem unusually happy people, enjoying everything they do, but sometimes they are not as happy inside: they hide more secrets, both good and bad, than other pigs.

THE LIFE CYCLE

HEALTH: Those born in the Year of the Pig are somewhat delicate, in line with their mild and gentle natures. They are vulnerable to illnesses of the stomach and intestines, and to food-related problems. Ordinary overeating can be dangerous for them, as well as the abuse of alcohol and pills. They are also sensitive to fluctuations in temperature and extremes of hot or cold weather, and susceptible to skin and eye problems. They should generally avoid heavy physical labor and exercise, and guard against the effects of stress and depression, although these will usually be temporary.

MONEY: Conservative and cautious in management and investment, pig people dislike taking big risks or throwing money around, for they are too aware of the dangers of temptation and the eternal ups and downs of the business cycle. They will tend to be defensive players in money matters, patient and hardworking, planning well and paying attention to timing, and many will be highly successful. Investments related to the element of Water, including anything involving nourishment, will be advantageous.

CAREER: Patient and intelligent, people born in this year are open to a wide range of professions. They may be artists, designers, educators, geologists, lawyers, doctors and health-care professionals, psychologists, scientists, technicians, or politicians. They may also find careers in management and finance, restaurants and the food industry, music, public relations, or visual communications and entertainment.

LOVE: Those born in this year are usually warm and romantic lovers, but unlikely to fall in love blindly. They may back off from a relationship that seems to be becoming too intense, withdrawing into contemplation. Their patience is extraordinary, but does have limits, and though they may tolerate encroachments on their territory for a long time, they will eventually get very angry if the situation does not change. These rages do not last, and with their fine sense of the absurd they are very forgiving in the end, laughing at their friends and lovers and just as much at themselves. Holding the last position in the zodiac, which carries the link to the new cycle, they are often gifted at joining fragmented emotions and mending and comforting broken hearts.

PIG PARTNERS BORN IN
THE YEAR OF THE...

MOUSE: These two gourmets will have a lot of fun together, going out and analyzing their meals. With their common interests and complementary approaches to life, they can make a whole that is greater than the sum of the parts. Mouse may want to feel intellectually superior to pig, but will not attempt to dominate it emotionally, and the pig who can get used to this will derive great personal benefit, learning in the process to be a little more aggressive.

OX: Though it enjoys pig's friendship, only the ox recognizes the pig's secret vice of stubbornness, and since the ox insists on being the fixed pole in any relationship, it hesitates to get emotionally involved. If they do become romantically linked, the pig may regret it, because the ox is much more stubborn and there will be a great deal of conflict.

TIGER: The pig is right to be frightened by the intensity of the tiger's possessiveness, but wrong to think there is no future in this relationship. Mutual attraction is based partly on the fact that these two are fundamentally good people, capable of learning to understand one another better if they give it time and attention.

RABBIT: It can be good for pig to be involved with rabbit, especially if the pig is the older party: it will have to take a more aggressive role than usual, deciding where to go and what to do and facing the rabbit's criticism if things are not just so. It can also be very good for the rabbit, but it may take longer for rabbit to realize this. Fun is at the center of what is going on, so it shouldn't be difficult for pig to summon the patience to see this game through to the end, which might be permanent romance.

DRAGON: Pig has nothing to worry about: in this affair, the dragon's unpredictability is just part of the fun, and the pig should sit back and let itself be entertained. The pig knows very well that nothing human is perfect, but this relationship comes close.

SNAKE: It seems like a shame that two such intelligent people should have so much difficulty understanding one another, but a snake and a pig who stumble into a relationship will most probably find themselves unable to communicate. The pig finds itself uncharacteristically rigid and angry, and it will be very hard, if not impossible, for anything positive to develop.

HORSE: This is at best a bumpy relationship from the pig's point of view. The horse probably feels things are going very well, and nothing the pig says has any effect in changing the situation. It may be wisest for the pig to cut its losses and leave, but love and wisdom are not necessarily compatible.

RAM: The pig involved with a ram should ask itself whether it is really serious, or simply coasting because nothing else is happening. The pig rarely hurts anyone on purpose, but can wound the ram inadvertently with innocent gestures that, to the ram, imply a commitment that is not there. If there is a real commitment, the pig should make this clear.

MONKEY: This can start off as a highly satisfying physical relationship; the pig is rather shocked by some of the monkey's naughty ideas, but enjoys them tremendously. If it lasts longer—that can be the problem with monkeys—it gets better, acquiring more and deeper emotional qualities. It will be worthwhile to give this relationship time to develop.

ROOSTER: No relationship with a rooster is easy, and especially for the pig, who doesn't feel like making an issue out of being treated with respect. The rooster is probably more in love than it lets on, however, and deserves to be given plenty of chances to reform.

DOG: The dog snaps and growls, but its heart is as good as the pig's, and they have a lot in common. Friendship is the best part of this relationship, but not the only one. Given a chance to develop, it covers all the bases of love, and there are few romances that allow the pig to feel so secure and so excited at the same time.

PIG: Nobody understands one pig as well as another. When they first meet they stay up all night talking, each amazed at the other's sensitivity. After awhile this perfect communication may start to seem routine, and one of the two will begin wondering if that's all there is. It's a lot, however, and more than many people ever attain.

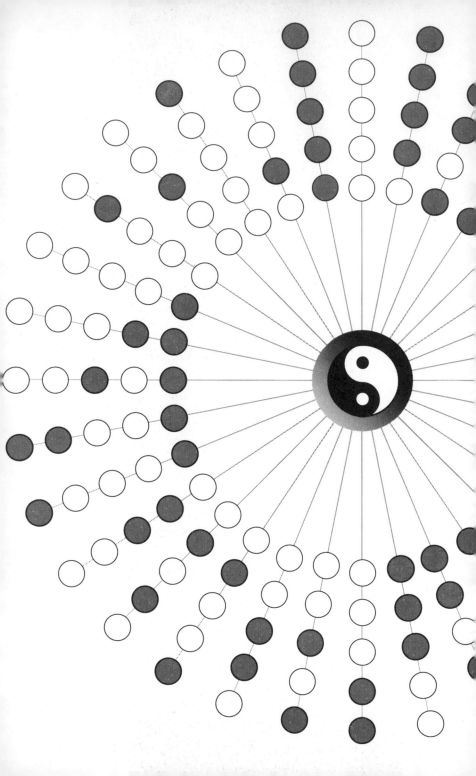

THE
YI JING
COIN
ORACLES

THE
YI JING
COIN
ORACLES

The *Yi Jing* (sometimes spelled *I Ching*), or *Book of Changes*, is the classic text in the ancient Chinese tradition of divination. The sixty-four oracles contained in this complex text reveal the deepest mysteries on all matters through a series of 384 secret messages. At some point, perhaps toward the end of the Song Dynasty in the twelfth century, the essence of these messages was distilled into thirty-two verses for the purpose of a simpler divination procedure using five coins. These thirty-two verses, known as the Yi Jing Coin Oracles, are still used as simplified symbolic representations of the principles contained in the *Yi Jing*, translating its wisdom to reflect on different aspects of the human condition in response to specific questions.

In consulting the coin oracles, the first requirement is for you to establish an environment of calm, concentration, and intimacy with ·

the matter in question. Then ask a single question, or, at any rate, focus on one question at a time.

Select five coins of the same denomination (e.g., all nickels or all dimes, but not a mixture) and place them in a bowl or cup, or in your two hands. Shake them gently but thoroughly. Close your eyes, relax, and focus on the question you want to ask. Shake the coins again, thoroughly and gently. Keeping your eyes closed, or at least not looking at the coins, arrange them one by one horizontally on a table in a straight line.

Then, open your eyes and note the heads-and-tails pattern of the five coins, left to right. Using the chart on the following page, match the coin pattern with the number of the verse. Turn to the correct page, check the diagram of the coin pattern, and then read the verse and its interpretation. Caution: these are metaphorical and symbolic answers, and therefore open to a wide variety of possible readings.

Be sure to ask no more than one question for each arrangement of coins, and never ask more than three questions in a single session.

THE YI JING COIN ORACLES

Find the pattern of coins you have thrown;
the numbers indicate which verse to consult.

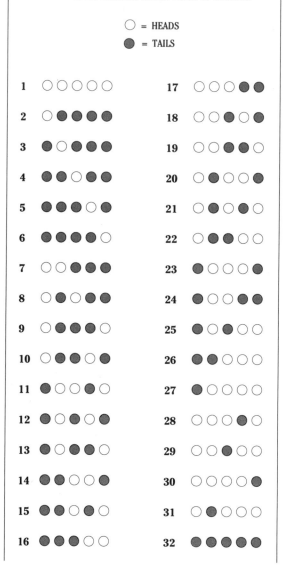

○ = HEADS
● = TAILS

1 ○○○○○   17 ○○○●●
2 ○●●●●   18 ○○●○●
3 ●○●●●   19 ○○●●○
4 ●●○●●   20 ○●○○●
5 ●●●○●   21 ○●○●○
6 ●●●●○   22 ○●●○○
7 ○○●●●   23 ●○○○●
8 ○●○●●   24 ●○○●●
9 ○●●●○   25 ●○●○○
10 ○●●○●   26 ●●○○○
11 ●○○●○   27 ●○○○○
12 ●○●○●   28 ○○○●○
13 ●○●●○   29 ○○●○○
14 ●●○○●   30 ○○○○●
15 ●●○●○   31 ○●○○○
16 ●●●○○   32 ●●●●●

186

VERSE 1 ○○○○○

The colorful Phoenix of the East manifests its auspicious signs,
The Unicorn arrives at the royal court.
Good luck resides to ward off evil spirits.
The joy of happiness and peace is here

INTERPRETATION: The first two lines indicate that the most favorable and auspicious mythological creatures in Chinese folklore, the Phoenix and the Unicorn, are providing a favorable environment for long-term ideas, plans and projects. However, before you can have your happiness and peace, you must still ward off obstacles and evil spirits by putting things together in the proper way. Even with good winds from the right direction, you still need to set the sails and man the tiller for a successful voyage.

SUMMARY: Very favorable conditions; you will get your wish.

VERSE 2 ○●●●●

Soldiers in armor,
The time has come to change and move on.
The Carp leaps over the Dragon's Gate,
An ordinary person is transformed to an immortal.

INTERPRETATION: A very favorable verse. The first line, evoking an experienced soldier returning from the battlefield, indicates past effort, whether for good or ill. Being alive and in one piece is something to be thankful for. The second line indicates the potential for progress, a breakthrough, or a change of direction that may provide you with new challenges and better opportunities for attaining your long-awaited goals. The Carp and the Dragon's Gate of the third line are both good-luck symbols in Chinese mythology, but luck alone is not enough: to get anywhere the Carp itself must do the leaping. You must seize the opportunity in order to gain, symbolically speaking, the fruit of happy immortality, or contentment. The stress is on change and constructive action.

SUMMARY: The chance is very good your wish will come true.

VERSE 3 ● ○ ● ● ●

Wind creates movement,
Friends can provide help.
When you find your trusted person
Your mind will be at ease.

INTERPRETATION: The first line suggests an important activity or plan in the works, or perhaps sudden progress toward a long-standing goal or desire. However, the key is the trusted person; there is some particular advice or direction needed before what is being sought can be satisfactorily obtained. The trusted person may also be information sources or portents of direction that signal to you as clearly as the voice of a trusted adviser. But there is no reason to be anxious; the winds propelling you are generally favorable, and progress will be made with or without outside assistance.

SUMMARY: Your wish will probably be realized as soon as the proper conditions are met.

VERSE 4 ● ● ○ ● ●

A boat floating on the lake,
Treasure to be found on the beach.
Your potential can be further expanded,
Good luck will come to disperse the bad.

INTERPRETATION: The slightly satirical verse indicates that some of your ideas and plans have been floating toward the accomplishment. The second line hints that the wandering boat is bound for hidden treasure waiting to be discovered on the beach under the sunny blue sky. The third line suggests that certain conditions are required before your goal can be reached; you must extend your potential to enhance your chances. The implication is that ambition has its risks, and there is a price to pay before you reap the reward. This is reinforced by the fourth line, providing encouragement in the face of obstacles or unhappy experiences you may already have encountered. Good luck will come through further effort and further trials. Information and connections may be what is required. In the end, you may find what you want.

SUMMARY: Your goals are ambitious, but not impossible, though you may need to modify them and exert extra effort before they are attained.

VERSE 5 ●●●○●

This oracle points to the south,
A great danger is coming.
Do not engage in arguments or disputes;
Trouble could happen in front of your eyes.

INTERPRETATION: In specific cases, this verse need not be feared; it does, however, warn of the need to play it safe and proceed with caution. In the first line, the south is not to be taken literally; it is a metaphor for safety (sunny and warm, kind and friendly), and taking a defensive rather than risky approach to your affairs. The key concept is that of patience: lying low to weather the storm, one learns to persevere against adverse conditions. Even at the point when grave danger is to be faced, be alert, calm, thoughtful, and secure in the knowledge that you have protected yourself. The third line makes it clear that even amid provocations and disputes, you must see things in perspective and wait for the right moment. Hold your ground and avoid making the situation worse. Seeing the danger signs before your eyes, approach the situation soberly; stay away from temptations and addictions. Wait for adverse winds to blow over and you will be on safe ground again.

SUMMARY: Be wise, cautious, and patient. Give things plenty of time and room.

VERSE 6 ●●●●○

Take a scholarly position,
Do not listen to unwise words.
Be cautious and be careful
Make a good luck wish to preserve your tranquility.

INTERPRETATION The first line indicates something important is in progress or about to reach a critical point that may cause a good deal of anxiety and confusion. You should not be alarmed, or ashamed, or sad; this is how things develop. The best position is be objective and analytical, to see matters in perspective. As the second line indicates, there is lots of advice, wise and unwise, floating around, but in life anything can happen. Together with objective information and detached analysis, the caution and care mentioned explicitly in the third line are decisive elements in obtaining your goal. Having made your best efforts, be wise and calm. Make a good luck wish to preserve your own harmony and balance of the yin and yang, and be thankful that you have put your wisdom to good use: whatever the result, you are fine!

SUMMARY: Be objective and measured. The matter you ask about can go either way. Maintaining your balance and harmony is itself a success!

VERSE 7 ○○●●●

When a nation is well managed,
People will be prosperous.
Accumulating wealth to enhance happiness,
Having health is equivalent to luck.

INTERPRETATION: The first line is a metaphorical reference to important actions or long-term plans whose successful outcome is indicated in the second line. Your intentions are crucial to the attainment of the goal, since it depends on your attitude, skill, and performance. There is also an indirect hint that you are discontented or ambitious for more, or are perhaps worried that something going smoothly may suddenly turn bad. There is tension and stress in the background. In the third line, wishes for prosperity are expressed, but accumulated wealth may not enhance happiness, personal peace, and satisfaction. The *Yi Jing* constantly reminds us of both sides of the picture, the concrete versus the abstract, the material versus the spiritual. The last line provides consolation in the truth that good health and serenity are as valuable as material success in the attainment of happiness. The key indication is the importance of your choice of attitudes and actions in the achievement of your goal.

SUMMARY: With favorable conditions, your wish will come true. Be aware of your own intentions, and be thankful.

VERSE 8 ○●○●●

Heaven grants all the graces;
Open the door to let in happy air.
Soon a helping hand will come,
You will be joyous and have all the good things.

INTERPRETATION: The first line indicates that mother nature has given blessings to all, and opportunities aplenty; action is underway, or an idea about to take shape. The second line encourages this process to develop further: let in the air and fortunate thoughts to enhance the opportunities for attaining your goal and to generate stamina for the long-distance run. The helping hand of the third line can be renewed energy, a fresh piece of advice or information, or perhaps a person or event that serves as a catalyst—but will be available to you only as long as you keep the door open to growth and to new choices.

SUMMARY: By allowing new growth, your wish will come true.

VERSE 9 ○●●●○

Trees are still in winter sleep,
Leaves are gone and there are no flowers.
Look, spring is around the corner;
Gradually buds will start bursting.

INTERPRETATION: The first two lines suggest an idea, plan, or activity at a standstill or in a long transition period. But this quiet and lonely state is part of the nature of things. It is a time for self-preservation and planning, redefining and reassessing the situation, preparing for the favorable time to come. As the second part makes clear, the active phase of the eternal cycle will soon arrive, and there will be plenty of time for action when new things start to happen, like spring buds bursting on the branches. The key is patience and positive planning.

SUMMARY: Be patient and prepared; your stored energy will help you get a good start when the time comes, and your wish will eventually come true.

VERSE 10 ○ ● ● ○ ●

The favorable time has come,
Things asleep will be resurrected.
With the addition of moisture and drizzle
Spring brings along new growth.

INTERPRETATION: The first line announces the end of a period of difficulty or obstruction. A favorable time is arriving, and, as the second line says, it provides an opportunity to revive dormant ideas and projects. The last two lines clarify this with the metaphor of the spring rains—water, as always, symbolizes prosperity—that nourish the growing things that have hibernated through the winter. The advice is to seize the opportune moment when things are ready to sprout, by taking action guided by appropriate planning.

SUMMARY: Look out for new possibilities and take action at the proper time; your wish should come true.

VERSE 11 ● ○ ○ ● ○

Disaster is dispersed and the door of good luck opens,
Much happiness and joy will come.
Soon you will meet someone,
An unexpected gift.

INTERPRETATION: The first line suggests a breakthrough after a long period of deadlock. The second line characterizes this moment as very auspicious. The last two lines explain that the breakthrough comes through the agency of something—a person, an action, or a piece of information—that you did not count on or perhaps even suspect. It is a positive change in direction, like an unexpected gift arriving just at the moment of greatest need.

SUMMARY: When the opportunity arrives you will almost certainly succeed.

VERSE 12 ●○●○●

Improvement and advancement will reward the neglected scholar;
He will change his plain dress for an embroidered robe.
For the person who receives this oracle,
Everything will be fine.

INTERPRETATION: The first line refers to the literati of old China, who used to spend years of their lives studying for the Imperial Civil Service examination, often in conditions of severe poverty. If they passed the examination, they were appointed as court officials and mandarins, symbolized by the embroidered robe in the second line. Advancement in the imperial government was not, at least in theory, through family connections or class background, but purely on the basis of educational qualifications. The first two lines thus represent a long and arduous struggle toward an ambitious and noble goal. The last two lines make it clear that the oracle does not apply to scholarship alone, but to any question that is asked. They encourage you to adopt a positive attitude and to hope that your struggles will soon be rewarded with honor and happiness.

SUMMARY: If your effort is well planned and prepared, it will certainly succeed this time.

VERSE 13 ●○●●○

Sitting at the bottom of the well to see the moon,
You grasp only shadows, not form.
Wealth comes and goes,
Be cautious and wise to preserve tranquility.

INTERPRETATION: The first two lines suggest the danger of acting on misinformation or subjective observation, and jumping to conclusions without considering the overall situation carefully. This kind of difficulty can come from within, or from outside sources; either way, it may lead to illusions and disappointments in life. The money matters of the third line are symbolic of any kind of change, offer, project, or desire for success: things come and go in constant cycles. It may not be wise to make a quick decision at this time, for there is the danger of losing your balance. The key is to be sober, resisting greed and avoiding danger.

SUMMARY: Weigh your wish carefully and objectively, and gather all the facts before you make your move.

VERSE 14 ●●○○●

Your mind and thoughts are in contradiction,
So are the results of the events.
Patience is a virtue;
Safeguard your actions and stay away from trouble.

INTERPRETATION: The first line indicates that you have arrived at a dilemma, contradiction, or deadlock of indecision. This will affect the results of your actions, as the second line says. The problem may be a mixture of various factors, and it can be resolved, but you will have to be patient. Take things step by step, regroup and redesign to coordinate your ideas with your desires, and especially avoid provoking actions that may further complicate the situation. This is easier said than done, but that is the point: it is a challenge to learn the wisdom of patience and control. Meanwhile, once the storm has blown over, sunny weather will come again, so there is no reason to rush now and regret later.

SUMMARY: Your wish may be confused or overly ambitious, and you may need to rethink. Be patient and stay out of trouble.

VERSE 15 ● ● ○ ● ○

A barren tree against snow and frost,
A lonely boat in the midst of a storm.
Scared, feeling quite helpless,
Does every step seem blocked?

INTERPRETATION: The frightening picture conveyed by the first two lines still leaves room for hope. The tree may be leafless in the winter weather, but it is not dead; the boat is threatened, but not sinking. The message is that you may be experiencing rough times, or else hard times are about to arrive. Scary and difficult as they may seem, they will be temporary. If you feel blocked at every step, you may need to relax so you can see more clearly; take the time to think and plan ahead, and devote your energy to weathering the storm. Conversely, if everything is fine, don't forget that the good times, too, are cyclical, and use your strength and wisdom to prepare for trouble.

SUMMARY: Be prepared and exercise judgment; do not panic or feel helpless, because there are more possibilities than you may think.

VERSE 16 ● ● ● ○ ○

The sun rises on the eastern sea,
Filling the world with brightness.
When actions and usefulness are in harmony,
Everything will be successful.

INTERPRETATION: The first two lines suggest that an early start, in the appropriate context, can be beneficial and beautiful. With the warmth of an enthusiastic attitude, your energy will penetrate in all directions, like the sunlight. Along with the idea of earliness denoted by the sunrise, the mention of harmony in the third line also suggests the importance of timing: to be in harmony, action and its goal must be well-timed with respect to each other, making the goal attainable. You should beware of procrastinating; an early move is indicated.

SUMMARY: To make your wish come true, good attitude, hard work, and proper timing are required—and the best time is the present.

VERSE 17 ○○○●●

All the obstacles are gone,
Good luck begins to come,
Like a night traveler walking in the dark
With the moon coming to illuminate the way.

INTERPRETATION: The first line refers to efforts and plans that have made no headway, a frustrating and disappointing situation. But the situation is changing, as the second line announces; perhaps a connection will be established or a new piece of information come to light. The new opportunity may come like moonlight in the night, guiding you on the path to the goal. But the second two lines also remind you that the moonlight and the path by themselves are not enough: you have to keep walking. Timing, direction, effort, and dedication all combine to enhance the chance for success.

SUMMARY: Keep going and working hard; things are going to change for the better.

VERSE 18 ○○●○●

Taking medicine to restore health,
The illness lingers.
Be careful and conservative in all other matters;
Make a good luck wish for a peaceful mind.

INTERPRETATION: The situation suggested by the first two lines could be a troubled relationship, a dispute, a career problem, or business deal—anything that seems to be dragging on endlessly in spite of your efforts to rectify it. The problem can interfere with other parts of your life as well, if not handled cautiously, patiently, and tolerantly. Human life is like water, finding its level eventually, but taking different courses to reach the sea. After you have done your best, be relaxed and cultivate a sense of humor; your way may not be perfect, and you should be careful not to make matters worse. In any case, there is no need to rush. Make a good luck wish for yourself, sit back and analyze the situation objectively, and preserve your peace of mind.

SUMMARY: Be cautious, don't insist; keep your sense of humor.

VERSE 19 ○ ○ ◐ ● ○

This oracle is on an uneven path,
Like rust eating away the inside of a copper coin.
Deep thoughts and worries cause regrets;
Human affairs may not always be harmonious.

INTERPRETATION: The first line indicates a period of many ups and downs in your life or the particular matter at hand. The coin of the second line is a traditional Chinese copper cash, with a hole in the center to hold it on a string of coins. This means that rust can attack it from the inside, as your problems can damage you psychologically. The third line, therefore, warns against excessive worrying. As the fourth line says, life is not a fairy tale, but very complicated and multifaceted, and people's desires and behavior may not always harmonize with each other. Insight and wisdom—and a sense of humor—are needed if you are to make it through these bumpy times; perhaps you should consider lowering your expectations.

SUMMARY: Your wish may be unrealistic; be wise and take it easy, or reorganize your plans. There is no need to subject yourself to so much stress.

VERSE 20 ○ ● ○ ○ ●

Strong roots give birth to good branches and leaves;
In a dense forest the trees grow in different shapes.
When things are going well,
Even the fragrant orchids can prosper like weeds.

INTERPRETATION: The first line expresses the familiar truth that a good beginning or foundation provides what is necessary for strong growth. But the second line reminds us that not all growth takes the same form; a healthy ecology supports diversity. These two lines are a warning against authoritarianism and forcing conformity to a single model. The whole tone of the verse is very auspicious, full of references to things thriving. It suggests a favorable moment, now or about to begin, when delicate orchids grow like wild weeds, meaning that under your care even the weakest factors can prosper. But you must take care not to lose your sensitivity to the eccentric and the fragile when this lucky period begins, and to allow everything to express itself in its own way. Be thankful for your good fortune.

SUMMARY: Chances are your wish will come true, with happiness and prosperity for all around you; but guard against abuses of power at this happy time.

VERSE 21 ○ ● ○ ● ○

Fame comes with position and power,
The dragon and the phoenix find their own ways.
Even with all one's wealth and possessions,
It is beneficial to travel afar.

INTERPRETATION: The first line suggests that the attainment of very ambitious goals is possible or imminent; this is a very auspicious oracle. The animals of the second line are the Green Dragon of the East and the Firebird of the South, and they are compared to the person whose desire for power and prestige has been granted. Such a person is in a position of influence, has more options than others, and is free to work toward a personal goal. It will be wise for the happy few with such privileges to add knowledge and spiritual substance to what they have already accumulated. The voyage referred to in the fourth line is a spiritual journey, at the end of which you will learn to recognize the fundamental absurdity of power and wealth.

SUMMARY: When you attain all your wishes, be wary of your own ignorance and do not abuse your power. Try to acquire wisdom.

VERSE 22 ○ ● ● ○ ○

Full moon in a clear sky,
Its brightness illuminates tonight's happy feast.
Every family is grateful for the good celebration;
Within ten thousand miles not a trace of cloud.

INTERPRETATION: One of the most auspicious times in the Chinese calendar is the Moon Festival on the fifteenth day of the eighth lunar month, when families gather for dinner and mooncakes to commemorate the goddess Chang E, who became immortal by stealing her husband's elixir and fled to the moon to escape his anger. The full moon on this night is the roundest and brightest of the year, and you can just about see her in the silver palace, with her companion, a rabbit forever milling medicinal herbs with a mortar and pestle. Life on the moon can be lonely, but life on earth can be marked by warm and happy family gatherings. The suggestion of the verse is that you have reached a moment when you can afford to relax, keeping your mind free of worries, like a cloudless night sky.

SUMMARY: The best thing you can do about your problems at this time is to forget them for a moment. Relax and take time out to celebrate life.

VERSE 23 ● ○ ○ ○ ●

To have fortune is to have health;
Having fame will enhance prosperity.
When all goes well the scent of precious orchids fills the air,
Sensed everywhere throughout ten thousand miles.

INTERPRETATION: The first two lines subtly suggest a distinction between ordinary good fortune, the kind that is equivalent to fame and enhances prosperity, and real good fortune, equated with health, not as easy to attain or to appreciate when we have it. The verse does not really say what you should or should not do, leaving the options more or less open. It implies that all is going well, and an aura of well-being may be felt all around you, like the fragrance of orchids wafting across great distances. The happiest and best time in your life may be here, or about to arrive. The quiet suggestion is that you concern yourself not so much with the attainment of wealth and fame, but with health and self-control.

SUMMARY: When you reach your luckiest time, take charge of your health and be wise.

VERSE 24 ● ○ ○ ● ●

A tired horse is about to start another trip,
A hungry person has to travel another long journey.
The obstacles ahead are plenty,
Not much room to lean back.

INTERPRETATION: One may interpret this verse is as a forewarning of what may happen if an obstinate person persists in ignoring a situation and pushes forward relentlessly. If you are the obstinate person yourself, you should consider the feelings of those you drag along, like the tired horse and the hungry person, and give them a break. You, too, must prepare for obstacles, leaving yourself enough room to lean back, retreat, and rest. If you are the tired and hungry one, you should take this advice all the more to heart in view of the struggles and hard work that lie ahead. Either way, anger and resentment will come if the situation is not addressed. Perhaps it is time to reflect, reorganize yourself after a rest, and try again, with a different goal or tactic. But do not try to gain more than is possible: you can't lose more than twenty-four hours in a day, and you can't gain any more than that either.

SUMMARY: Save yourself and others excessive stress. Pause to readjust your goals and ambitions.

VERSE 25 ● ○ ● ○ ○

The Trinity is your companion,
Auspicious light is shining through.
Conditions are favorable to further your creativity,
Your chance will come naturally.

INTERPRETATION: The Trinity in the first line refers to the Chinese gods of Good Luck, Wealth, and Longevity, and the first two lines say that they are watching out for your well-being. The second two lines suggest that now is the time to reach further into your creative energies and bring your dreams to fruition. The chance will arrive even though you may not have asked for it, but you still must work hard to take advantage of it. The whole verse hints that you are fully capable of realizing your dreams when the opportunity presents itself, as long as you mind your environment, and practice skill and self-control.

SUMMARY: Good luck and hard work will bring you to your goal, and your wish will come true.

VERSE 26 ● ● ○ ○ ○

This oracle arrives at six points of harmony,
Bringing plenty of luck and good wishes;
Like a wandering traveler returning home,
Humming a joyous song and feeling happy inside.

INTERPRETATION: The six points of the first line are the directions North, South, East, West, up, and down. The indication is that harmony prevails everywhere, inside and out; this is a very auspicious oracle. The second two lines refer to a goal that is a type of return, whether a literal return home or a regaining of stability and the feeling that you are where you have always belonged. The journey has been arduous and long, but you are now within sight of the end, and a happy song bubbles out of you at the sight of the familiar landmarks you have been longing for. The message is that now is no time to give up, or even rest; you should not let your energy flag at this point, when your goal is so near and the circumstances so favorable.

SUMMARY: Chances are your wish will come true; do not stop at this point, because happy days are on the way.

VERSE 27 ● ○ ○ ○ ○

Good rain delights the young seedlings,
Why fear a poor harvest?
Let your mind alone to be happy,
Be comfortable, and don't worry.

INTERPRETATION: The first line suggests that a well-planned effort has been made and will come to fruition in a natural way, as the rain coming at the expected time nourishes the fields that have been properly planted and weeded. The rain in this case may be the helpful agency of a friend, a piece of information, a new offer, or whatever; it will come at the right time, and no sooner, so there is no point in worrying about it. Of course it is right to be on the alert for hidden dangers, but once you have done your best and the seedlings are planted, it is all right to rest and enjoy a few happy moments. The effort you have made is already a success in its own right.

SUMMARY: Success will come at its own pace; be at ease, you are doing fine.

VERSE 28 ○○○●○

Still quite a distance to go in the middle of the journey,
Clouds encroach and the sun sets behind the mountains.
Frightened, looking for a safe place to stay,
Dangers ahead and behind.

INTERPRETATION: This is a verse whose symbolic message needs to be interpreted by indirect thought and questioning. The first two lines set an ominous scene to alert you to obstacles or unexpected dangers that can come up at any time. If you are on the road late in the day and a storm is approaching, you must find a place to spend the night, and smart travelers are those that have timed the journey so that they reach the inn at dusk. Similarly, for any long-term plan, you must not try to make so much distance on a given day that you find yourself beyond reach of shelter, and you should be prepared for dangers and difficulties that are not on the agenda. Be alert, present, and mindful; it is enough of a challenge to be strong. Don't take too many risks at this point, and watch your step.

SUMMARY: Your wish may be too ambitious; be conservative, alert, and think things over before going further.

VERSE 29 ○○●○○

Pearls come from within an oyster,
Jade is concealed in a rock.
Make a contribution to barter for good luck,
Troubles will not turn into disasters.

INTERPRETATION: The first two lines suggest the frustration of working hard without seeing any results, indicating an effort toward a goal that remains hidden, like the pearl in the oyster or jade in the quarry. It reminds us that just because we cannot see the thing we are working for does not mean that it is not there. We should not yield to disappointment or prejudging the situation superficially. The third line makes the familiar point that fortune favors those who help themselves. To take action or make an effort is an offering, and its reward will be better luck in the future: a breakthrough to the hidden desire, or at least aid in preventing minor problems from growing into catastrophes. You must make an effort to discover new ground; the situation may not be as bad as you think.

SUMMARY: Keep trying, and do not prejudge the situation; give it another look.

VERSE 30 ○○○○●

The Celestial army punishes bandits,
Returning home with victorious banners.
Rewards will be given to generals and soldiers;
Families will share their honors as well.

INTERPRETATION: A very happy and favorable verse. After turmoil and misunderstanding, a chaotic situation is about to be resolved at the end of a long struggle and much effort. The Celestial army, the good guys, drive away the bandits, or evil influences, to restore balance and harmony. The last two lines remind us that not only the leaders will be rewarded for their contribution, but also the humblest foot soldiers, as well as their families. It has not been easy. The price in hard work and sacrifice may have been very great, but the result is proportional to the effort.

SUMMARY: Your hard work will pay off and your wish will come true.

VERSE 31 ○●○○○

Thinly padded shoes walking on ice,
Crossing over a dangerous bridge.
Layers of trouble you have come through;
Beautiful spring is coming to you.

INTERPRETATION: The picture of a cold and dangerous passage through a wintry landscape hints at a difficult and challenging period in your life, but the last two lines advise you not to give up hope. Indeed, you have suffered much pain and frustration, emerging from one difficulty to find yourself in another, as if your troubles were layered on top of one another, but in the end everything will be well. Spring is coming, in the form of a breakthrough, a helping hand, a valuable connection that will revitalize you in progressing toward your goal, as spring weather renews the earth. Be patient and keep your hopes up.

SUMMARY: Despite obstacles and dangers, your wish will come true; it has not been easy, but the struggle will end.

VERSE 32 ● ● ● ● ●

> Bronze coins buried in earth and dust,
> Precious jade fallen into mud.
> When will they come out again?
> To display their beauty.

INTERPRETATION: Perhaps your work, personality, health or ideas have not received proper attention, or have been altogether ignored, like precious things, Chinese coins or pieces of jade, lying undiscovered and neglected. The third line suggests that this is only a question of timing. The circumstances may not be right just now, but you need not question your own value as a person. Someone will come along and realize your worth, picking up and treasuring your good qualities like a piece of jade plucked from the mud. You must be patient and hopeful about present dangers and obstacles, and carefully preserve yourself for the coming breakthrough and recognition. Perhaps, too, you have been neglecting yourself; you need to rediscover your own good qualities and have more self-esteem.

SUMMARY: Do not neglect yourself; you may be surprised by the treasures hidden within you.

SELECTED BIBLIOGRAPHY

Birch, Cyril. *Chinese Myths and Fantasies.* London: Oxford University Press, 1962.

Chartrand, Mark R. *The Audubon Society Field Guide to the Night Sky.* New York: Alfred A. Knopf, 1991.

Chen Pin Hong. *Bian zheng bai nian li* (Annotated hundred-year Chinese lunar calendar). Taipei: Jing Kang, 1986.

Cheng San Feng. *Shi er sheng xiao cha min yun* (The twelve Chinese Zodiac signs and fate reading). Taipei: Modern Age, 1980.

Christie, Anthony. *Chinese Mythology.* Middlesex, U.K.: Hamlyn, 1968.

Clark, D.M. and F.R. Stephenson. *Application of early astronomical records.* Bristol, 1978.

Edward, T.C. *Ancient Tales and Folklore of China.* Bracken, 1922.

Hackin, J., et al. *Asiatic Mythology.* New York: Crescent, 1963.

Hook, Brian, ed. *The Cambridge Encyclopedia of China.* Cambridge: Cambridge University Press, 1982.

Ju Bao Liu tong shu (Ju Bao Liu Chinese almanac). Hong Kong, 1985.

Larousse Encyclopedia of Astrology. New York: MacGraw Hill, 1980.

Li Hua. *Ba gua chung-heng* (The Eight Trigrams and their meaning). Beijing: Tuan Jie, 1991.

Li Ti Bei. *Yi Jing zhan bo pan gi xiong* (*Yi Jing* oracles and their decisions of luck). Hong Kong: Guo Feng, 1989.

Menzil, D.H. and J.M. Pasachoff. *A Field Guide to the Stars and Planets,* 2nd ed. Boston: Houghton Mifflin, 1983.

McHenry, Robert. *Liberty's Women.* Springfield, Mass: Merriam-Webster, 1980.

Nakayama, Shigeru. *A History of Japanese Astronomy.* Cambridge, Mass. Harvard University Press, 1969.

Needham, Joseph. *Science and Civilization in China.* III, IV. Cambridge: Cambridge University Press, 1954-.

Routledge and Kegan Paul. *Folktales of China.* London, 1965.

Si Lin Shan Ren. *Su yu xue quan ji* (Complete book of fate calculations). 2nd vol. Hong Kong: Sing Sing, undated.

Smith, Richard J. *Chinese Almanacs.* Hong Kong: Oxford University Press, 1992.

Waley, Arthur D. *Monkey* (translation of the 16th-century novel *Xiyouji,* by Wu Cheng-en). London: 1973.

Webster's New Biographical Dictionary. Springfield, Mass.: Merriam-Webster, 1988.

Wei Nin Jai Zhu. *Zhi Mi Dou shu yi mun* (Introduction to the Big Dipper school of fate calculations). Hong Kong: Hong Kong Astrological Society, 1990.

Welteran, Bruce. *New York Public Library Book of Chronologies.* New York: Prentice Hall, 1990.

Werner, E.T.C. *Myths and Legends of China.* London, Hanap, 1922.

Williams, C.A.S. *Outlines of Chinese Symbolism and Art Motives.* 3rd ed. Shanghai: Kelly and Walsh, 1941 (reprinted New York: Dover, 1976).

Wieger, Leo. *Chinese Characters.* (Trans. from the French by L. Davrout.) 2nd ed. Catholic Mission Press, 1927 (reprinted New York: Dover, 1965).

Wong, C.S. *An Illustrated Cycle of Chinese Festivities in Malaysia and Singapore.* 2nd ed. Singapore: Jack Chia-MPH, 1987.

Wu Gui Tang tong shu (Wu Gui Tang Chinese almanac). Canton: 1890.

Yi Tong. *Shi er sheng xiao shou ce* (Handbook of the twelve Chinese zodiac signs). Hong Kong: Hong Kong Astrological Society, 1990.

ABOUT THE AUTHOR

KWAN LAU, born in Hong Kong, is a trained architect specializing in architectural acoustics. An ordained Buddhist priest, he is also a scholar of classical and modern Chinese literature, history, and the arts, and internationally known as a pioneer collector of nineteenth-century photographs of China, Japan, and Tibet. He lives in New York as an artist and writer.